— THE —
STORE

Memoir by: Neil DeFillippo

PAGE PUBLISHING, INC.
Conneaut Lake, PA

First originally published by Page Publishing 2021

ISBN 978-1-6624-3124-1 (pbk)
ISBN 978-1-6624-5102-7 (hc)
ISBN 978-1-6624-3125-8 (digital)

Printed in the United States of America

ACKNOWLEDGMENTS

SALLY PUTNAM CHAPMAN and Jack Chapman, thank you for seeing the possibilities of the story as I ran the facts of it by you both. Sally, with the writing of your own book, *Whistle Like A Bird,* about your grandmother, you were able to show me a valuable insight into my own story. Jack, with your vast experiences in media, the two of you were people whose opinions I greatly appreciated.

Adrian Spratt, thanks for reading the first rough draft of *The Store* and making what I feel were wonderful criticisms and saying that also you felt I could be a good story writer. With your vast experience in writing and your exceptional intelligence, I tried to practice what you suggested.

Diane Montagnoli-Frissora and her husband, Ralph, thank you for being true friends, giving to me all the help I needed in doing and redoing the story and refining it all and your encouraging words along the way.

Emily Figueiredo, thank you for spending your summer vacation from college to help make changes to my story. Whatever tasks I would ask you to perform, you never hesitated to say, "No problem," which was very important to me. Thank you also to your parents for being so helpful and raising such a special daughter.

To everyone at Page Publishing, especially Andy Saksa, for making the journey into having a book published such a pleasant experience. I can't thank you enough!

Kayla Camille Seftner, my beautiful granddaughter, thank you for doing the rewrite at an early stage in this venture while still handling your college chores. Grandpa loves you and is very proud of you.

To my dear friends Charles and Franchesca Biondo, thank you for pushing me forward with your encouraging words and deeds. Charles, thank you for helping design the front cover along with your team at The Biondo Group. You listened to what I wanted and because of your expertise in your field simply said, "That's easy."

To my daughter, Lydia DeFillippo-Seftner, words aren't sufficient to express how important you have been in seeing the book through its final words. Without your unbelievable work with the publishing team, this book would have never come to fruition. As I was truly a duck out of water when it came to getting things needed by the publisher done on my computer, and thankfully, Lydia, you did such an extraordinary job that even the publisher's team was in awe.

Finally, to my wonderful wife, Camille, thank you for your patience in my writing of this book. Papers all over the house, never complaining but understanding through the four years how important this labor of love was to me. I love you! God Bless you always.

INTRODUCTION

"THE GLUE THAT solidly held our family together had dried up and been washed away by the currents of the Atlantic. Not through anyone's fault, it would never be the same again."

Being one of four grandchildren still alive, I should, in fact must, write this book about our very special grandmother, Cristina Covino, and *The Store* that was such a special part of our lives. There were thirteen grandchildren in total. Somehow, she made each of us feel special, and yet in fact we were all different. She loved us unconditionally, whether we did good or not in school or other endeavors in our lives. She would, however, give us a dressing down when we got out of hand to the extent that she thought was beyond tolerable. When Grandma would say to us in broken English "What do you thinka you doing? Making a disgrace to youselfa and our family. Grandma wantsa you to stop," somehow in most cases that was the end of our being out of control. She had spoken and we listened.

She would tell us that you can sometimes buy fake love with money but never respect. She felt respect to people is the way you got respect back. Those that didn't respect you back, you should cut those ties with them and move on. The word respect was very important to her. She would say, "They hava no respecta."

She lived what she said, always showing respect to family, friends, and customers. Maybe that was what made her such a successful and admired person and business-woman. You will see Cristina, her family and friends in the story that follows, warts and all. We never looked upon her illegal business as something that she was but just some-thing that she did, having no part in the grandmother she showed to all of us.

When a customer who had in her mind a little too much to drink, she would cut them off. No swearing of any kind was allowed in The Store. If someone uttered a curse word, she would take out a very large butcher's knife that she kept next to her slicing machine and, pointing it to the individual, would say, "I cuta your tongue out of your mouth," which she never had to do. The other peo-ple that the individual came in with apologized to her and would usually escort him out. I don't know if it was because they loved the taste of the liquor or just respect; they didn't want to not be allowed back in The Store. Occasionally she would have strong muscle guys from the Bronx come to the store, pulling up usually in Cadillacs entering the store while customers were there. Going behind the counter, they would all give her a kiss on the cheek. Then usually climb-ing the four steps into the living quarters, saying hello to what other family members were there. After a short while they would leave, the seed had been planted, and the word spread among customers that Mom, which they called her, wasn't one they should disrespect.

CHAPTER 1

Who Was She? Where Was She Going?

CRISTINA DIPALO WAS born in the town of Fragoli outside Naples, Italy, in 1888, a town that was dominated by petty thieves who took advantage of the local people plus anyone passing through. If your bike was left alone for any amount of time, you would return to find it missing. In some instances, the thieves would offer to sell it back to you. Cristina would never ride to town and instead would walk almost two miles from her home and back to avoid giving up anything that belonged to her. This attitude continued throughout her life, not being afraid to work hard to protect what belonged to her whether it was her children or the business she had created—the store.

Her brother John had left for America in 1902 at the age of eighteen. Their father, Donato, was a barber and a dentist for the town. John learned to be a barber at an early age. He had gone to America after his mother died giving birth and his dad remarried. The children didn't get along with their stepmother, who didn't treat the six of them well. This hastened John's departure.

Cristina was amazed by the many things John wrote her about the new country. When her father decided to immigrate to America, Cristina was thrilled. However, he and his new wife took along only Cristina and her sister Emily (Molly), leaving behind his son Ferdinando (Fred) and two daughters, Julia and Luisa, who were put into a home for children without parents. Fred and his sisters were treated terribly as were most of the other children in the home. Fred was abused both physically and mentally because he would act out when he felt injustice was occurring.

The trip across the Atlantic was harsh. Steerage was where most of the Italian immigrants, including the DiPalo family, were lodged as this was the least expensive accommodation. The first few days were pleasant as the sun shined brightly, bringing people up onto the deck from below where the stench was almost more than Cristina could take. People were packed in with very little hygiene available. Toilets were limited; and the crew did little, if anything, to improve the conditions. It then started to rain and continued for a week. The situation below became worse than before because the heavy rains and winds kept the people from going up on the deck. Dysentery became a huge problem, and some of the infants below died.

When the weather finally got better, the people in steerage went up on the deck and stayed there until the ship docked in New York at Ellis Island, refusing to go back below despite the order to do so by the captain. When they departed from the ship, Cristina was exhausted both physically and mentally. She followed her father around like a trained seal, following him as he went from station to station, being disrespected by the customs officers who made crude remarks and had no empathy for these new immigrants who arrived mostly from Southern Italy.

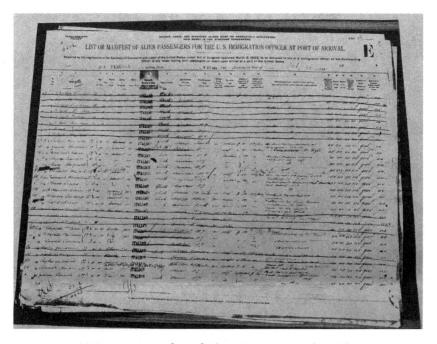

SS Perugia Manifest of Alien Passengers, when The DiPalo Family sailed to America—1904

CHAPTER 2

New Country, New Wonders, New Beginning

ONE OF CRISTINA's cousins was waiting for them as they cleared customs. He brought them to an apartment he had rented for them in Lower Manhattan at 118 Mulberry Street, an area known as "Little Italy" as it's still called today. Though much has changed since they moved there in 1904. Cristina was amazed by the amount of people living in such a small area. The pushcarts lining the streets selling anything you could possibly need from underwear, fruits, vegetables, fish, meats, Italian delicacies, pots, pans, and the most valuable item—ice. Ice was carried up to the apartments by the icemen with tongs or on their shoulders. The ice was placed in an icebox which was put out the window of the apartment to keep the perishable items from going bad. You name it, you could get it on Mulberry Street. Even an organ-grinder with a monkey holding a tin cup to receive money as the man played the accordion. What amazing sights for a girl who was sixteen years old.

The area was then, and to some degree still is, controlled by the Mafia. You had to pay them to operate just about any business. They kept the people living their intimidated by their ruthlessness. The area has made much progress since Cristina lived there. It has become well-known for the finest Italian restaurants, imported foods from Italy, cookware, statues, and desserts. It was also well-known for where many of the Mafia could be seen at restaurants, on the streets, or in espresso cafés. No business could operate without consent from the Mob. You either paid them for the privilege or made them a partner. In other instances, they would open a business in someone else's name. The Feast of San Gennaro had started and became well-known throughout America. People flocked there every summer to get a taste of Italy. A small portion of the feast money went to the local church with the rest of the proceeds going to the wise guys that operated it. In the last few years, the feast has lost a great deal of its "pizzas." Many of the blocks inhabited by Italian Americans is now inhabited by Chinese American immigrants.

Cristina's brother John was living in Brooklyn, New York, and was aware that the family had arrived from Italy. Even though his relationship with his father and stepmother was strained, he would go to Mulberry Street on Sundays to see his sisters. That was his only day off from being a barber. Having learned the trade in Italy, he had become a master barber with a good following. After saving enough money, he opened his own shop. His shop did very well not only from his expert workmanship but from John's outgoing personality. Many of his young friends that had arrived in America in the late 1800s or early 1900s as he did were hard workers and enjoyed going to his shop on Saturdays when they were off from work to get a shave and shoot the breeze. Some of his friends were up-and-coming members of the Mafia in Brooklyn which, later in Cristina's life, became a key element in her success. John was a meticulous dresser with a very fair complexion and light hair. Each week that he went to their apartment, his sisters would tell him of the terrible ways the stepmother was mistreating them. He talked to his father about this several times, but nothing was ever done to improve the situation. Finally, one Sunday, he got into a heated argument with his father about how things were. With this, John told the girls to pack their bags, which was one suitcase each with their belongings. Their father could not stop him as John was a very strong young man, and according to Cristina, the father didn't seem to care if they left.

There was a cousin who, along with his wife, had a boardinghouse in Yonkers, New York, a suburb of New York City. They were in need of help to keep the place in good condition. Yonkers at the time was coming into its own as an industrial city. This was because a large part of it was on the Hudson River, allowing it to easily ship goods to most of the East Coast. It brought immigrants there since it was in need of workers—some skilled and others were laborers. The workers there were primarily Polish and Italian. A boardinghouse was very much in demand as those people, mostly men, needed a place to stay. The two sisters, Cristina and Molly, were responsible for cleaning the rooms and helping to prepare a light breakfast in the morning and dinner which was served at 6:00 p.m. sharp. The boarders had to have a job as rent was due every Sunday. No rent money, no room on Monday. There were plenty of men waiting to rent.

One of the boarders was Emilio Covino, a good-looking, smooth-talking young man. He was a blacksmith by trade but had also become a singer, sewing machine repairman, and salesman, driving his horse and buggy to many homes and farms in the area to service and sell sewing machines. When he first saw Cristina, he was immediately taken with her beauty. After exchanging small talk with her from time to time, he asked her cousins if he could have permission to court her. When they replied in the affirmative, the young Emilio started talking to Cristina about his hopes and plans for the future. She was sixteen in 1904. Her brother John gave his permission for the two to get married. Emilio was twenty-two at the time, being born in 1882.

Current photo of 118 Mulberry Street apartment where
Cristina first lived when she arrived from Italy in 1904.

Current photo of fire escape at 118 Mulberry Street where
Cristina and her family lived on the third floor.

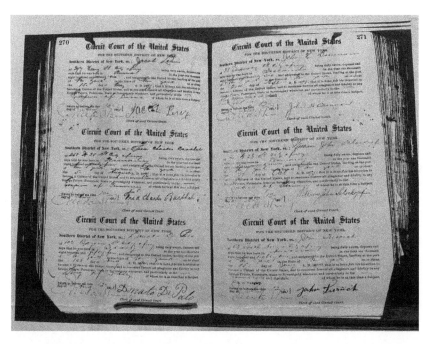

Donato DiPalo (Cristina's father) documentation for Citizenship—1907

CHAPTER 3

Young and Aggressive

AFTER A SMALL wedding given by Cristina's brother, the young couple moved into an apartment above a row of stores in Mount Vernon, New York. Life was good for these two Italian immigrants. They saved much of the money that Emilio made. The business was growing rapidly, and he gave up being a blacksmith to concentrate solely on the sewing machine business. In 1906, their first child, a boy, was born. They named him Nicholas (Nick). A daughter followed, who was named Rose. After that, the family moved to a larger apartment on South Seventh Avenue. The area was inhabited mostly by Italian immigrants. Therefore, the businesses were run by people who spoke fluent Italian. Although, not all of them were Italian themselves. They learned to speak the language in order to survive. It, in some ways, felt like living in Italy.

Whatever foods were needed for Cristina to prepare for her family were readily available. She shopped every day for her husband, two children, and herself. There was no such thing as refrigeration as we know it to be today. The birth of Rose in 1908 was not the last by these very much in love couple. In 1910 came Filomena (Fannie); 1912, Olga; and 1914, Lydia.

Emilio worked long hours—getting up at 6:00 a.m., going to the nearby stable, hooking up his horse to the buggy he owned, and, with the lunch Cristina made him, was off to conquer the world. His route went from Mount Vernon to White Plains, an area with homes and farms that predominantly were owned by immigrants who were able to provide for their families and, at the same time, to grow produce to sell to the public on a sometimes-large scale. Most houses and farms along Emilio's route had a sewing machine or needed one whether it was to make new clothes for the family or repair older ones. Also, to make every-thing from drapes to tablecloths, pillowcases, blankets, etc.

A mother's work on a farm was truly never done, work-ing late at night after everyone else in the family was fast asleep. While many of the men worked their farms, some had gotten jobs that had sprung up in the factories or mills in Westchester County. In that case, when they went to work, the women would take over the farming chores as well. The one thing missing for many of these women was getting attention from a man. This area today has become dominated by car dealerships, furniture stores, and various other businesses. Gone are all the farms that were a main-stay well into the early 1940s.

Emilio would arrive back home as it got dark. There, his wife would be waiting with a hot meal, a glass of wine, and later espresso with something she baked earlier in the day. Cristina would bake every day. The children were not allowed to have dinner until Emilio sat at the table. They had a small piece of whatever Cristina baked that day when they got home from school. Then it was homework and study until their dad got home.

Emilio dealt almost exclusively with the women, which was fine with him, as he had an "eye for women." Because of his good looks and a gift of gab, many were happy to see him when he would visit their farms. His children would often say, "He could sell the Brooklyn Bridge." He was considered a "Dapper Dan," having not only one horse-drawn carriage but a second one with a fringe on top. On Sundays, he would take the family out in it and visit relatives and friends. Emilio also was very active in his church, Our Lady of Mount Carmel. Each year, the church had a Saint Anthony's Day parade. The men would carry the statue of the saint throughout Mount Vernon, being followed by men playing Italian marching songs on their very large instruments. People would stop by the saint and place dollar bills on it as a way to thank God or to pray for a blessing. Marching out in front of the statue was Emilio with his spats, straw hat, and cane, strutting like a proud animal. He was the leader of the procession for many years.

The women on the farms would have him sit and offer him espresso or a glass of wine, which would become a problem for him later in life. In some cases, conversation would lead to touching and then intimacy. Stories started to come back to Cristina about his fooling around. She wasn't a woman who would sit back and take this behavior. Lydia, the youngest daughter, heard the arguments between her parents in regard to her father's infidelity. The arguments almost always ended with Emilio sweet-talking Cristina and denying affairs, claiming the people who were spreading these rumors were jealous of his success. He was so successful that by 1915, Emilio was able to buy a home on Railroad Avenue in Mount Vernon. As the years went by, the rumors continued.

Cristina's main concern was her children, making sure they were well-mannered, cleanly dressed, and that they did well in school. She impressed upon them the importance of education. Cristina herself was an avid reader. This showed in part by naming her last two children with Russian names from a book she read on Russian aristocracy. She felt education was the door that would open you to success in America. Cristina thought it would wipe away the stigma and prejudice of others that Italians were only good for using their backs for work as they had no brains. She would show the people who felt that way how wrong they were. Her son Nick graduated from high school at the age of sixteen and was employed at First National Bank as a teller. He became head teller at the age of eighteen, which at the time was a very prestigious position. Olga was a supervisor at New York Telephone by the age of nineteen. Lydia was a ferocious reader, spending most of her free time at the library. Later in life, her husband, Jimmy, would go out on Sunday mornings to buy her the *New York Times* so she could do the crossword puzzle. Rose and Fannie both married before they finished high school, which made Cristina quite unhappy.

Nick was quite a man. Becoming head teller, he was excellent at math which came so naturally to him. In fact, some of his friends who were in college would ask him to tutor them. Later in life, these friends became doctors, lawyers, and, in one case, mayor of Mount Vernon and later Westchester and New York State Supreme Court justice. Nick was great to talk to, soft-spoken but very learned about any subject. It was very seldom that anyone could remember seeing him without a white shirt on. While married and with children, he continued his education at night, going to night school and becoming a CPA. In the 1950s with the construction business booming, Nick was the CPA for some of the largest construction companies in New York State. Some of the owners of these companies would not make financial decisions without consulting him first. He was never heard uttering a swear word. His sisters loved him dearly and would often say he was an "angel." He very seldom did anything to upset his family; instead, he would be a calming voice until the 1950s. Then unfortunately, things changed because of a situation involving money in the family. There was much more at that time that disrupted the Covino family.

Meanwhile, previous to all that in 1924, a woman came to the Covino family's door. When Cristina answered the door and didn't recognize the person, she asked her what she wanted. The woman said she was looking for Emilio because she was his girlfriend. That was the last straw for Cristina! She left him the next day, taking Olga and Lydia with her, leaving Nick and Fannie with Emilio. Rose had already been out of the house having married Harry (the

Horse), who lived on East 214th Street in the Bronx. Lydia was ten years old at the time, and Olga was twelve. For an Italian American woman to leave her husband in those days was almost unheard of. It was more like whatever the man did had to be accepted. Cristina, however, was no ordinary Italian American woman. She moved into a small one-bedroom apartment on Eighth Avenue in Mount Vernon. She paid the rent with money she had squirreled away over the years. When the money ran out, Emilio paid the rent for her and the girls and asked her to return home. Her answer was emphatically no! She refused, knowing in her mind he would never change. His children wanted to go home as they loved their father dearly. When the family was together, he would shower them with gifts, laughter, and love. Cristina told people that she had not five but six children with Emilio being the sixth, never growing up.

Cristina called her brother John and told him what had happened and that she left her husband. He wasn't surprised knowing her inner strength from when she was a small child, going through many hardships to the present. He knew she would survive. The only question was, doing what. Although she was an excellent seamstress, he didn't want her to work in what was called a sweatshop as the women and, in many cases, underage children were abused physically and mentally. As she had a good way with people, he felt she would do well in some kind of retail business. A grocery store selling Italian and American food would be an ideal venue.

They looked around the south side of Mount Vernon as that was where many of the Italian immigrants had settled.

There was also a spattering of Black families living there. They had come from the south and were looked upon as cheap labor. Cristina and her brother found a store with rooms behind the store and an apartment on the second floor that she could rent. She and John went and talked to Emilio to see if he would give her money to purchase the building. They explained that Olga and Lydia needed a bedroom for themselves as the three of them were sharing a single bedroom. The building was $1,800. The year was 1925. Emilio didn't have the money in cash, but loving his children so, he sold his house on Railroad Avenue. Between what he got for his house and the money he did have, Cristina was able to buy the building at 424 South Seventh Avenue. This would be Cristina's very first venture into real estate but by no means her last.

Current photo of Mount Carmel Church, Mount Vernon, New York

CHAPTER 4

Groceries to Booze

1926

AFTER MUCH CLEANING and painting, the store was ready to open in the summer of 1926. There was one small problem: Cristina hardly had any money to buy the items she needed to sell. A salesman came around and, after meeting her, decided he would give her credit. The store opened with whole provolone hanging in the window from the ceiling for all to see. The cheese had bags attached to their bottom so the oil that came out of them wouldn't go over the floor. There was also prosciutto hanging, large burlap bags filled with espresso and Central American coffee beans that would be ground up in front of the customers, pastas placed in glass drawers, Italian bread brought in fresh daily, eggs in cartons, and milk in glass bottles, etc. As late as the 1940s, provolone and prosciutto were still hanging in the window. By then however, they were there for the family to eat rather than sell to customers. The taste of the sharp provolone with tomatoes, the Italian bread, and a glass of wine is a feast in itself. The taste of prosciutto, which is a sweet Italian ham, is to die for. Of course, it must come from Parma, Italy, where the climate for curing is perfect. Although it sells anywhere from fourteen to seventeen dollars a pound, the taste cannot be matched by any other prosciutto.

Lydia in 1926 was twelve years old, and Olga fourteen. The girls used scoops to fill the orders of coffee and pastas. Most of the buying came from Italian immigrants in the first two years. Also, in 1926 Fannie, the second-oldest daughter, eloped with Louis (Copey). This was after a tumultuous courtship. It reached the breaking point shortly before the couple eloped. The Covino family was attending a wedding that Fannie had been a bridesmaid in. Louis (a.k.a. Copey) and some of his friends crashed the wedding as they had not been invited. Copey tried to take Fannie out of the wedding. A fight broke out; and he, along with his friends, created chaos with women screaming and children crying. Copey punched a cousin of Cristina's named Pasquale (Patsy). Patsy pulled out a knife and cut Copey down the right side of his face, the scar of which remained with him for life. Patsy ran away to New Jersey where he stayed for a few years.

The bad feelings between Copey and his mother-in-law, Cristina, continued for many years. However, as time often does, healing was accomplished between these two very hardheaded people. Copey turned out to be an excellent provider for his family. He and Fannie had five wonderful children, one of which died at a young age in a tragic accident. Copey passed away after a hard day's work as a steam shovel operator from a stroke at the age of fifty-two. Patsy went on to play a very important part in the saving of one of the Covino girls' life.

In 1927, the makeup of the area changed, where many Blacks came from down south as the word spread that there were jobs available in Mount Vernon, New York. The word was spread by the Blacks living there to friends and relatives. Cristina saw the opportunity for new business. She started selling foods that Blacks liked to eat, such as okra, collard greens, chitterlings, even fresh catfish that were kept in a tank. Here was one minority group, the Italians that, at the time, were a minority in Mount Vernon serving another minority, which was in a city run and controlled by people of mostly German and Irish ancestry.

The increase in job availability for Blacks was because of the coal companies, starting up between Fulton and Columbus Avenues going East to Boston Post Road. The jobs needed physically strong men who were able to unload the barges with the coal that had come through the waterway. They then had to be loaded onto horse-drawn wagons to be delivered to Westchester County and the Bronx where many factories and homes were being built.

Cristina's brother John would stop by the store quite often to see how business was going. "He came all the way from Brooklyn," Lydia would say quite often, which in those days was quite a trip! Seeing how good business at the store had become, he suggested the clientele was great for selling alcohol too—wine to Italians and corn, gin,

NEIL DEFILLIPPO

and rye to Blacks. There was only one problem; that was Prohibition! It had started in 1920, and selling liquor was illegal. John understood that was the situation. However, people had a desire to drink alcoholic beverages, and no law was going to change that fact. Coming from Italy and relocating to Brooklyn, New York, many of his friends had, by this time, become part of the Mafia hierarchy. Telling Cristina of the high rate of profit and his connections, she decided to go ahead with his proposal. John took Cristina to Brooklyn where she met some of his friends who controlled large parts of the illegal alcohol business. They told her how it would work. The alcohol would be delivered late at night to avoid police problems in what was called "tins." It would be transported by small trucks that could fit up the driveway on the side of the house, then put into the garage in the back of the house. They had been given the layout of the house by her brother. Cristina was told the alcohol business in Westchester was handled by Jewish mobsters that the Mafia had an agreement with.

They put Cristina in touch with a chemist in Manhattan that would supply her with the flavors to make the liquor to be sold to customers. They would also deliver to her a barrel of wine to be sold to the Italian customers. They told her she would be given credit, not having to pay for the alcohol for thirty days and without interest. Interest was a big part of the Mafia business then as it still is today. Lending money with very high interest is called "shylocking." The word had been used by the Jewish people dating back before Christ. This changed the store in a radical way starting in the fall of 1927 when Cristina became the first

30

large-scale woman bootlegger in Westchester County, New York!

Lydia, whose bedroom was on the driveway side of the house, would hear the trucks during the very early morning hours delivering the tins of alcohol. She or Olga would take the trolley from Mount Vernon to the East 241st Street train station in the Bronx, then the subway to Manhattan. The time of the trolley and train ride combined took about one and a half hours each way. Upon exiting the train, they would then walk four blocks to the apothecary which was owned by the chemist. Sometimes Lydia would bring Rose's daughter Tina with her. A fourteen-year-old girl with a younger child never attracted any suspicion. They would enter the business and go to the back. The chemist would give them the packages of flavors, and they would pay him. This continued into the forties when United Parcel would deliver it. Cristina was up at 5:30 a.m. six days a week and 8:00 a.m. on Sundays. During the workweek, the girls would be up at 6:00 a.m. to help make sandwiches, most of which were sold to Black customers before they went to work. The men worked very hard at the coal yards. As late as the fifties, there were still some, but not many, coal yards in the area as the main source of heat had become oil. Cristina would serve them one glass of liquor before they went off to work, but only one. That was her policy during the week. Being a smart businesswoman, she realized that if they couldn't work properly, it would open a can of worms that she wanted no part of.

As the Italians started doing better financially, they were able to buy their own homes and make their own wine in their basements. That part of the business started to "dry" up. However, more people heard of the quality of Cristina's liquors. They came from as far away as White Plains, which was about twenty miles, and all parts of the Bronx, especially on the weekends. You could go into the store but only three people at a time. They had to stay in their cars until someone left. That was where they could buy a glass of liquor for fifty cents. It was three times more volume than a shot. The grandchildren were responsible to keep the traffic moving on the weekends, starting in the 1940s, by telling the customers to go around the block and return after asking the customers what they wanted in either half or full pints. They then paid the grandchildren, went around the block, and would find their order waiting for them. I guess the Covino family were the first to have a drive-up liquor business. As business was booming in the twenties, Cristina's son Nick made sure that respect was paid to the neighbors of the store as they could make things very dicey for the business if they started to complain to law enforcement. In the later years, he instructed his mother to pay all her taxes on any moneys taken in. For it had become the one way you could be sent to prison for a long time.

The business continued to do well in 1928, so much so that Cristina needed help mixing the alcohol and moving tins to the place where it was hidden. Fred, her brother, would fit the role perfectly. The only trouble was he was still living in Italy. He tried to enter America legally in 1924, but when he arrived at Ellis Island, he was sent back to Italy because of poor vision. In those days, if customs didn't think you would be an asset to the country, they would send you back. Cristina was adamant that her brother was who she wanted to help her. She would find a way to get him to America! Cristina reached out to the Mafia in Brooklyn and asked what she could do. They told her there was a sea captain who went back and forth from America to Italy that should be able to help her. It was known in the underworld that for the right price, he could bring someone in illegally. They would set up a meeting for her at the store. Lydia remembered the captain coming to the house where he and Cristina discussed the price. They agreed on the price of $1,500. The only fly in the ointment was that he wanted to be paid in advance. Cristina said, "No way." In those days, it was quite common for people to pay in advance and never receive what they had paid for. Being in an Italian home, he was served espresso and a piece of her pizza dolce, which was a sweet pie made with ricotta cheese that must be moist. This was done by adding liquor to the pie as it was being made. Lydia remembered him eating two pieces. Not saying this was what closed the deal, he agreed to not taking any money in advance. It would strictly be paid on delivery.

Before Christmas in 1928, Cristina received the phone call she had been praying and waiting for. The captain called and said he had arrived in New York, and he was in possession of her "package." Late in the evening, a friend drove her to the west side pier where the captain's ship had docked. Cristina got out of the car and paced back and forth for what seemed forever, when it was only about fifteen minutes. Suddenly, she saw two men walking toward her—one was the tall captain, the other was a man about five feet, eight inches tall. He had tears in his eyes. The first words he said were *faccia bella* (beautiful face). Ever the businesswoman, she handed the captain an envelope which he opened, counted, and he said *grazie*. Cristina said to him, "You brought me back a part of my life." She then started to cry as she and brother Ferdinando (Fred) hugged. The two of them sat in the back of the car as they headed to Mount Vernon and the store.

Upon arrival, they were greeted by Olga and Lydia. After Fred hugged them and pinched their cheeks, they went into the kitchen where the two girls had prepared some food, which included prosciutto, provolone, tomatoes, hard-crusted bread, along with red wine. Fred couldn't get enough of it fast enough. This was by far the best food he had eaten since leaving Italy. When espresso was brought to him with biscotti, Fred recounted his journey to the three of them. During the trip, he was kept in the coal area, inhaling dust almost constantly. He was escorted up to the deck late at night where he could breathe fresh air. Each morning, he was given a piece of bread with a cup of coffee. In the evening, he received whatever was left from the officer's mess. The trip across the Atlantic was very unpleasant with Fred being seasick most of the time. He kept repeating to himself that the journey would soon be over, marking the days on the wall with a piece of coal.

When he would sometimes complain about the dust from the coal or looking for more to eat, he would be told by members of the crew that they could throw him overboard and he wouldn't have to complain anymore. However, these were just idle threats as the captain had his eye on the prize which was the $1,500 he was going to receive from Cristina.

Being a clever woman, Cristina found out from others that dealt with the captain that the going rate for smuggling in someone was actually $1,000. Not that she liked overpaying; she felt the extra $500 would go a long way to guaranteeing her brothers safety.

CHAPTER 5

Ferdinando—Fred and "Sonny"

FRED ARRIVED WITH much mental baggage. The years he spent in the children's home took its toll. He was physically and mentally abused. Fred became hardened and started to physically abuse young children in the home as he was no match physically to react against those abusing him.

Upon arriving in America, he became totally committed to Cristina, doing whatever she asked of him without questioning it. He took out his frustrations on the dogs Cristina had which were there to protect the business from any unwanted visitors, beating them whenever they started barking for what he considered no good reason. He also took out much of his anger on Rose's son Alfonso (a.k.a. Sonny), who had been left with Cristina as a small child. Rose had three children: the oldest, Rita, who went to live with her father's parents and Tina, who Rose kept with her. Many nights, Rose with young Tina would ride the train from East 241st in the Bronx all the way to Manhattan just to have a warm place to get some sleep. This was done so she wouldn't have to go to a shelter, where it was dirty and extremely dangerous.

All this happened because Rose's husband had been in and out of jail. He was never a provider even when he wasn't in jail, leaving her destitute and unable to provide for her children. Whenever Sonny would misbehave, Fred would take him down to the wine cellar that he had built and beat him and locked him in there. This went on for many years until Sonny was a teenager. Lydia was the only child of Cristina still living at the store who witnessed much of this cruelty. Sonny loved Lydia very much, and she felt the same. She had taken care of him from when he was a baby. Lydia did whatever she could to protect him from Fred.

He joined the navy as a teenager, but his time in the service didn't last long. He was discharged early as he had trouble with taking orders. All through his life, he seemed to want to be something bigger than he really was, and that created many problems for him throughout his life.

Sonny was a loving older cousin to me as I was growing up. He put a bushel with the bottom cut out on the streetlight pole outside the store and taught me how to play basketball. He would let me help him bring up into the kitchen the five-gallon green glass jug filled with wine when he really didn't need my help. He would always say to me, "I couldn't have done it without your help," just to give me something to be proud of myself for. He was twelve years older than me but treated me as an equal. He was very intelligent and a whiz at math. I feel Sonny could have been whatever he wanted, but he just seemed to always take the wrong road.

The store in 1928 experienced its first federal raid. There was a loud banging on the front door, which was kept locked. The people outside were yelling that it was the Feds and to open the door. Cristina was sitting in her rocking chair at the top of the stairs. She yelled to Fred, Olga, and Lydia what was happening, in Italian of course. The three started dumping the gallons filled with liquor down the sinks in the kitchen and bathroom, plus the toilet. The tins that had raw alcohol in them were quickly put into a hiding place in the store that was never discovered over the years by the law. As the Feds broke through the front door, they rushed up the steps past Cristina, who was still sitting in her rocking chair.

A pint of liquor hadn't been thrown out; Olga quickly hid it in the piano. However, the Feds found it and put it on the kitchen table and marked it. Then they went into the living room and asked Cristina to get up and escorted her into the kitchen. Lydia, who was not quite fourteen, thought to herself, *If I could work my way to the table and knock the pint of liquor to the floor, the Feds would have no evidence.* As she described, she inched her way toward the table, getting closer and closer. A Fed saw what she was up to and said, "Little girl, that is federal property. If you so much as touch it, I have the right to shoot you." With that, he opened his jacket and exposed his gun. Cristina, who had been taking English from a private tutor since 1927, understood some of what the Fed was saying and then, upon seeing him expose his gun, yelled at Lydia to get away, which she did. The Feds had no idea how large a business in illegal liquor the store was really conducting. Cristina was arrested and brought to a federal jail, where she got out quickly because all they found was one pint.

CHAPTER 6

Depressed Family to Depression to Opportunity

IN THE SUMMER of 1929 with the sun setting, Cristina's brother Fred was driving a Packard car that his sister had bought. A young boy ran across the street and was hit by him. The boy was rushed to the hospital by ambulance; however, his life could not be saved. Needless to say, his family was devastated and wanted action against Fred. As he was here illegally, it opened up many problems that Cristina paid his way through. Feeling terrible for the boy's family, she offered to compensate them for their loss in the boy's memory. However, Fred was put on trial for vehicular manslaughter. He was found not guilty by reasons that included the sun's glare and the fact that the boy ran out between two cars. He used to go to the boy's grave and put flowers for many years.

In 1929, the world was hit by the Great Depression, which lasted until 1941 when we entered World War II. The Depression affected just about everyone in the United

States in one way or another. In particular, it devastated Cristina's husband, Emilio. They never divorced. He was missing his children and wife and was spiraling downhill financially and emotionally. He was drinking too much wine and not taking care of his once lucrative business. After a while, he dropped out of sight from his children. In 1931, a woman that Rose knew had gone to the Bowery in New York City where many of the people down on their luck migrated to. She had gone there looking for her father but no luck. However, one of the Salvation Army shelters that she had visited was where Emilio was staying. Telling Rose, she and Fannie went to the Bowery and brought him home. He went to live with the Vitaliano Family.

Emilio was a welcome addition to the family. He walked the children to school almost every day and helped in whatever way he could. The entire Vitaliano family treated him with much love and affection. Emilio had a garden in the back of the house that was his pride and joy. Among the things he planted was a fig tree; it continued to produce the sweetest figs well into the 1950s. However, in the early 1940s, his health started to deteriorate. One night in 1944 he was rushed to Fordham Hospital in the Bronx, which was never known for great care. While at the hospital he fell out of the bed, hit his head, and died soon after. How much longer he could have survived without the injury is questionable, as he was in very poor condition upon his arrival at the hospital.

His body was laid out at the store in the living room, which was quite common in those days. After three days he was buried in a plot in New Rochelle, New York. The

Vitaliano family home where Emilio lived was a home Cristina had bought from a contractor in 1931 who didn't have the money to finish the project. He was directed to her and was told that Cristina might be interested and had cash to finish the project. She insisted he finish the home with money she would give him and would pay him after he submitted the bills to her, and her brother Fred looked over the workmanship. Then, and only then, she would give him the balance of what they agreed on as a total price. If he reneged in any way, the house would be hers as is. The contract was drawn up by a dear friend of her son Nick. The person was a young attorney at the time that later became a Mount Vernon judge then Mayor of Mount Vernon and then a New York State Supreme Court justice.

Meanwhile the Italian Americans were growing, canning, and jarring most of their food. The Blacks had their hours cut or lost their jobs entirely. Cristina's grocery store and alcohol business slowed down considerably. John suggested she should start taking illegal numbers. She declined and instead decided to build her own still in the Catskill Mountains. The problem was, she had to get the okay from her suppliers. They agreed but had to be paid a certain amount every month as compensation for allowing the still to be built. Cristina's son Nick went over the numbers and decided it would still turn out to be good for her. Fred her brother, along with some of their friends who were bricklayers, carpenters, etc., built a state-of-the-art still, for those days. Fred would make the brew starting in the early evening and, before it became daylight, transport it through rough and winding roads to avoid law enforcement. Fred had many perilous journeys through the Catskill and Adirondack area—everything from flat tires to, in one case, losing his brakes. One evening, while making the alcohol, he fell asleep; and the still blew up, nearly killing him. He remained with no eyebrows. That is how close he came to losing his life. The opened-back truck was loaded with the tins that had already been filled; and off to Mount Vernon he went, shaking almost all the way. When he arrived and Cristina saw the condition he was in, she was horrified! She called the family doctor who came to the store to treat Fred's burns.

He felt Fred should go to the hospital; however, Cristina asked him to do the best he could and please come back every day to continue treating the wounds. The doctor never asked how the burn occurred, having some knowledge of Cristina's business. He was the family doctor for many years; he knew that if Cristina didn't say anything about the details, it was better not to ask. The doctor did come by each day and treated Fred's wounds until they healed.

Current photo of Bowery Street where Emilio Covino
went to live during the Depression and was found there
by his daughters Rose and Fannie about 1931

CHAPTER 7

Using Muscle with the Help of Friends

AFTER THE STILL blew up, Cristina decided making her own alcohol just wasn't worth the trouble. Her brother, John, told her the people who had been in charge of alcohol in Westchester Country no longer were. It was now controlled by the mob from Arthur Avenue in the Bronx. She was put in touch with them, and for the remaining years that she sold liquor, they had a very good relationship. Many of the people from Arthur Avenue bought homes in Westchester County in the years going forward. This further solidified her relationship with them as they stopped by the store often to see how she was doing.

One problem that was taken care of when she first started dealing with the people from the Bronx was that the mobsters she had been paying when she put up her own still wanted her to keep paying them even though she was no longer producing her own alcohol. She explained this to the people from the Bronx. They told her not to pay anyone. The matter would be taken care of. Lydia said someone by the name of Amaduda, as she thought it would be spelled, came to the store personally, which was supposedly at that time a big deal as she remembered. He and Cristina went into the kitchen, and she made him a cup of espresso. Lydia and Olga knew even at their early ages not to go into the kitchen while the two of them were talking. That was the end of anyone coming to the store for money. She never discussed what she and Amaduda talked about, but it was obvious the power in the area was now controlled by the people from Arthur Avenue in the Bronx.

On another occasion, some young toughs from Mount Vernon came to the store and tried to shake her down. She, in no way, was going to give them money and told them so. Late that night, someone drove by and threw two bricks, shattering one of the store windows. Cristina knew she would have to take action! That resulted in her going to Arthur Avenue and explaining the situation. You never discussed anything that was "business" over the phone. She was asked where these young toughs hung out. Her children had told Cristina who and where they usually could be found. An upstairs poolroom in a store on First Street between Fourth and Fifth Avenue, which was where the young toughs hung out, was visited by strangers days after Cristina went to Arthur Avenue. The poolroom was busted up, as well as some of the people who were there.

The message was clear: don't ever go anywhere near the store again because the next time they had to come to Mount Vernon, the results would be worse. Word spread throughout the town that Cristina had extremely heavy muscle behind her. That was the end of that! Needless to say, no one ever tried to shake her down again. When you were a big earner as she was, by buying a large amount of alcohol, they would look out for you. That was true then and still is to this day.

CHAPTER 8

Depression Creates Opportunity

IN 1931, WITH her brother John's urging, Cristina started taking numbers. She turned the numbers into a family in a poolroom on Third Street in Mount Vernon. She also began giving credit to her Black customers with no interest added on. It was good business but also because she felt they had been very instrumental in her success. She knew they were hard workers and would do just about anything to provide for their families. She kept a record of anything bought by this group of customers, using only their initials in a ledger that the family called "the book." She would give credit only for essentials, such as milk, bread, butter, eggs, and vegetables. No way was there any credit given for soda or alcohol or playing numbers.

The number business was becoming very lucrative. This was because people had pennies, nickels, dimes, quarters—whatever they bet—having a chance if they hit to pay five hundred to one. The "New York" numbers, as it was called, was computed by totaling the numbers from the amount that the horses paid in certain races. The "Brooklyn," as it was called, was computed by getting the last three numbers from the total pari-mutuel handle at a particular racetrack. That number could be found in the *Daily News*, *Daily Mirror*, and many other newspapers every day in the racing portion of their sports section. Racing was a very important part of the sports page because it was the only legal gambling allowed in the United States at the time.

Those that she turned in to would pay off any hits, with her getting a percentage of any numbers she turned in. When she realized the money that could be made by being your own "bank" and since she had the financial resources to pay out on any hits, she decided to "book" whatever numbers were played with her. She already had a great reputation with her customers, paying them off the next day and sometimes that same evening as soon as the numbers were confirmed. Her good reputation also came from, in some instances, players who didn't realize they had a hit. She had their money waiting for them when they came in. Customers that didn't come in for a while would find their money in an envelope with their initials on it. Word spread that "Mom," as they called her, was 100 percent. When they brought in their "slip," she would write their numbers on a master sheet, giving them a copy in her writing, burning their slip. That way there was no question about what numbers they played, and just in case some would decide to add other numbers on to their own slip after they left.

After a while, other bookies started laying off some of their "action," if they had too much on a particular number with her. Cristina always took some of it, never more than she wanted to handle. Very seldom did she lay off some of her own action, although it did happen from time to time. This was one gutsy lady this Cristina Covino. To have, in some cases, large amounts on a particular number, she became admired by her fellow bookies. She kept her financial business to herself, while many of the bookies liked to brag about how they were doing and, in some cases, showed it with new cars and living the good life for everyone to see. You couldn't tell from looking at her whether she had ten dollars or a million. The same was true for her children—always low-key, never discussing money, especially in front of their children. The children were brought up to never ask questions about their grandmother's business or the family's financial situation. The children never heard their parents say anything disparaging about any relatives or friends. If they did have something not nice to say, it was never done in front of the children. That is why as children, they loved their aunts, uncles, and cousins so much and respected their friends' parents, who they never answered back if they were reprimanded by them.

Cristina had a tutor to teach her to read and talk in English. This started, as was said earlier, in 1927 and went on and off for three years. She felt that if success was to be obtained in her adopted county, it was essential to be at least somewhat literate in its language. A grocery salesman, who would come to the store to take her order for items she sold, would have long conversations with her about the wonders of America.

In those lean years of the early thirties, most of her customers would, at one time or another, send their family to get food on credit. Most of the time it was the children. The parents would say go to the store, which for them was only one place, and ask Mom, which is what they all called her, for this or that. In the "book," the amount would go next to their initials. Mount Vernon, being the closest suburban city to New York City, had many well-off people living there—bankers, stockbrokers, lawyers, judges. Also living just a few blocks from the store were the parents of baseball and New York Yankee great Lou Gehrig. Lydia said when the weather was good, the couple would walk past the store, and if she was outside, the two of them would say hello and continue their walk. Speaking of baseball, also living just a few blocks away was the Branca family, whose son Ralph became a pitcher for the Brooklyn Dodgers. He was a very good pitcher. However, he was best known for throwing the pitch Bobby Thompson hit for a home run in 1951—the shot heard around the world. That was one of baseball's most memorable moments. In 1928, Fannie had given birth to her first child, Cristina (Tina). In 1930, it was Gennaro (Jerry), and in 1932, Robert (Bobby). Fannie was a wonderful, loving person as I experienced many times in my life and especially in the forties and fifties. We lived in the same house, her family on the first floor and ours had moved to the second floor.

I could hear Fannie singing; she had a beautiful voice. I also remember her baking, which was second to none. When she baked, the aroma spread throughout the house. I think the singing and baking were great therapies for her and the rest of the family to help with the tragedy that befell them in the 1930s.

In 1931, Cristina made her first venture into the stock market. The grocery salesman that came to the store would also talk to her about the stock market. He would always have a newspaper with him and discuss the news of the day. He had been invested in the stock market and was practically wiped out in 1929. In 1931, Cristina asked him if he would take her to Wall Street as she wanted to invest. He was more than happy to do so. Lydia felt he was sweet on her mother and would do anything she asked. They took the train to Wall Street on what was her first, but not her last, trip there. Cristina bought stocks of several companies whose items she sold in her store. By the 1950s, those stocks had multiplied tenfold in their price. She felt this country would come back as it did. Lydia couldn't remember the salesman's name, only that he was Jewish and played a large part in Cristina's financial success and her love for her adopted country.

CHAPTER 9

Ice Cream to War

1936–1941

IN 1936, TRAGEDY struck Fannie's family and also affected the entire Covino family, who felt the pain for many years into the future. On a Sunday afternoon in the summer, Olga and her husband, Jimmy (Skinny Jimmy), who did not have any children of their own, decided to take Fannie and Louis's (Copey) son Bobby for a ride to get him ice cream. This was very common as they had done the same thing for many of their nieces and nephews in the past.

With his parent's permission, Bobby got into the car, and off they went. After about an hour, they returned to the store, parking across from it. Olga took Bobby by the hand, and they began to cross. Bobby saw his mother in front of the store with other family members. He broke loose from his aunt Olga and ran toward her. As he got to the opposite side of the street, a car driven by a doctor, who was going on a house call to a patient (they made house calls in those days), struck Bobby and dragged his body under the car. With everyone screaming, the doctor stopped his car. Jimmy and Copey crawled under the car and freed him. They laid his little body in the doctor's car; and off to the hospital they went, which was ten minutes from the store. The family, who were still screaming outside the store, went inside. Skinny Jimmy and Copey returned after about three hours, both crying, and said the doctors did all they could; however, they couldn't save his life. Fannie at the time was pregnant with her fourth child. She, along with her mother, Cristina, started to scream. The rest of the family was crying. Copey was holding his wife, trying to get her under control, which didn't work too well. She carried the scars of that day for the rest of her life.

On November 22, 1936, Fannie gave birth to a chubby, beautiful girl. In honor of their son, they named her Barbara. After that, Fannie was overly protective of her children, instilling in them fears of things that were in some degree a little risky but that other children experienced every day in their lives. They did, despite their fears, turn out to be wonderful people and great cousins. The fears were not only with Fannie's immediate family. Her sisters would repeatedly remind the other children in the family to be careful and to cross streets at the corners whenever possible, especially near the store. Even when driving cars, they were told to watch when turning at the end of the block. The children just listened with respect as they knew all the warnings came from love, remembering that terrible day.

In 1937, a friend of the family, Signor Bosche, who had quite a few friends in high positions in Italy, approached Cristina and told her a friend of his who was an Italian submarine captain was bringing his ship to New York. He asked if she would consider giving a party for them in the backyard of the store. She thought it would be exciting and something she would be happy to do. Of course, she paid all expenses for the party as Signor Bosche was great at planning parties but not so great when it came to helping to pay for them. In the 1940s, he would come to the store on Sundays for dinner, joining the family and some friends who brought their instruments with them. He was always well-dressed with a tie on. After dinner and quite a bit of wine, he would loosen his tie and start to sing Italian songs with everyone else joining in. Signor Bosche, with his hands, would conduct the friends who had instruments—which were a guitar, an accordion, a banjo, homemade instruments—and of course, with Fred playing piano. It was truly a great time that went on for many years, especially in the winter months as Cristina's friends were mostly in the construction field employed as bricklayers, carpenters, and laborers. There was no work for them that time of the year. Just to be together that time of the year with friends was very important to them.

The submarine arrived in June, and Signor Bosche escorted the captain and his crew to the store. In the yard, there were lights strung across and tables made of plywood, which were placed on wooden horses decorated with red, white, and blue tablecloths. There were a few very close friends, along with the family, that were also invited. Those that had instruments brought them along. Four sons-in-law carried the piano out of the kitchen and put it into the yard.

The captain and his crew arrived in the early afternoon and stayed into the evening. They dined on antipasto, salad, pasta with meatballs and sausage, then roasted chicken followed by Italian pastries and Cristina's cheesecake, then fruits, nuts, and plenty of wine. When they were about to leave, the captain invited Cristina to go to the west side pier in New York City and board his submarine the next day, which she readily accepted. When she arrived at the sub on Sunday with her son Nick, the captain greeted them and presented her with a bouquet of flowers. He then took her to the sub and then below deck. She was in awe of the inside of the ship. When she arrived home with the flowers in hand, she couldn't stop raving about her day. This hard-working woman, whose only thoughts for over ten years was of her family and running the business she had turned into a huge success, had a day to remember that was just for her.

In 1938 on January 4, I was born to my parents, Lydia and Jimmy. I was named after my paternal grandfather, sort of. It was a custom among Italian families to do that. My grandfather's name was Anello. My mother and father named me Neil because in those days, Italian people wanted very much for their children to assimilate into American society and to be accepted by their peers as Americans, showing that their loyalty was to the United States and not the land where their parents or grandparents were born. Some examples of their names are Giovanni

(John), Giuseppe (Joe), and Gaetano (Tom). Today many young Italian Americans, however, are naming their children with Italian names in recognition of the fact that Italian Americans are now totally accepted as a part of the overall society. Whether or not what the people did back in the day was right or wrong, they did it for their children to have a better life than they ever had.

I did not arrive without any problems. After my mom gave birth, she was in a semiprivate room at Mount Vernon Hospital. Also in the room with her was a woman who also gave birth. Sadly, the woman's child died while she was in labor. The event made her go over the edge mentally. While Lydia was resting, she felt someone hovering over her. Upon opening her eyes, the woman started to choke her. She fought and screamed for help. Nurses and assistants rushed into the room and pulled the woman away from her. Totally traumatized by that event, she insisted on going home immediately.

She went to the store as constant care had to be given to her. After a few days, her physical condition worsened. She was very pale and sleeping almost constantly. The family doctor by the name of Feldman was called. He found she was bleeding internally. In critical condition, she could not be moved and needed a blood transfusion. Lydia's sisters and brother Nick called relatives and friends and asked them to come to the store as fast as they could. As they arrived, they were asked for blood type.

A second cousin by the name of Pasquale (Patsy), the same person that cut Copey in 1926, was the same blood type. He was a big rugged man, a construction worker by trade. Patsy got onto the kitchen table. Lydia's room was directly across from the kitchen. The doctor hooked up tubes going from Patsy's arm into Lydia's; the precious blood flowed! Rose said later on, "You could see the color returning to Lydia's face and her eyes beginning to flutter." She was then transported to the hospital where the surgeons were able to stop the bleeding.

After a few days, she was able to sit up and was having her favorite food, Uneeda biscuits and butter, along with her coffee. I used to see Patsy and his family quite often at Grandma's on Sundays. In the 1960s, my family and I moved to Mount Vernon from the Bronx. My neighbors were the same Patsy that had saved Lydia's (my mother's) life years earlier and his family. He never mentioned what he had done for her. That was the way Italians were, feeling the people who they helped knew and that was good enough. Cristina was the same way, never saying what she did for people, which over the years was a lot.

Because of Lydia's condition, she couldn't breastfeed. Jimmy's (a.k.a. Fat Jimmy) sister Mamie had given birth to her son Peter at the same time Lydia had given birth to me. As she was breastfeeding her son, she volunteered to also breastfeed me. She was a beautiful, always-smiling person. Later in life when she and I were together with other people, she would say to them, "Isn't he so healthy and beautiful? He has my milk in him." She was loved by all that met her because she was a no-pretense person, who told you whatever was on her mind, without a mean bone in her body. One day when my wife, Camille, and I were in Atlantic City at a hotel, suddenly we heard a person yell out, "Neil, it's Aunt Mamie!" We rushed to her, and we embraced. That was, without a doubt, the best part of the weekend for Camille and me. We went to dinner with her and her husband and then had breakfast together the next morning. At breakfast we reminisced about many things our families did together when we were all younger. Aunt Mamie told me many things about my dad when he was younger that I wasn't familiar with. As I write this story I realize how much I loved her. Maybe there was more to her breastfeeding me then I ever realized before.

CHAPTER 10

Thanks, Fat Jimmy

JIMMY HAD MET Lydia when his family moved to Eighth Avenue in Mount Vernon, one block from the store. The family had moved there from the Bronx after the death of Anello at the early age of fifty-two. The family, with his father Anello, had lived in Harlem, New York, originally when they arrived from Italy. Because of all the fighting and shootings between different Italian American mobs, they decided to move. They went to live on 156th Street and Morris Avenue in the Bronx, thinking that area was safer for the children of which there were seven.

Jimmy was the oldest boy and; at the age of eleven, was taken out of school to help his dad, who was a junkman, with the heavy lifting that was necessary in that business. Meanwhile, the crime problem was a little better in the Bronx but not that much. As an example, one late afternoon while Jimmy's two older sisters, Mary and Concetta, were playing in the hallway of the apartment house where they lived, violence erupted. The front door flew open; and a man came running in, followed closely by another man brandishing a gun who fired multiple shots, killing the first man. The killer gave a long stare at the girls, and then opened the door and walked away. Mary and Concetta ran up to their apartment and told their mother and father what they just witnessed. Anello told them not to mention what they had seen to anyone outside the family. Two evenings after while the family was seated at the dinner table, there was a knock at the door. The mother, Jenny, answered it. The person at the door was known by many people in the neighborhood and recognized by Mary and Concetta as the person they had seen with the gun two nights before and was the shooter. He told Jenny his name was Vincent Cole, known in the area as Vincent (Mad Dog) Cole. He asked Anello if he could speak with him privately.

The two men went into the living room. Mad Dog told Anello if police would come by, he would appreciate it the girls didn't say anything. Anello assured him that would be the case and he would make sure the girls would cooperate. Mad Dog owned several of the apartment houses in the area. A short time after the conversation, Anello started getting jobs to clean out basements and empty apartments in several apartment houses in the area. Jimmy, who had been taken out of school, found himself working harder than ever.

In 1929 when the Depression hit, Jimmy did whatever he could to bring home money for the family, including working as a sparring partner in many of the local gyms. He also got into trouble with the law on several occasions.

During Prohibition in the twenties, he was driving a boot-leg truck for Dutch Shultz, a known owner of speakeasies in New York and a top-echelon bootlegger.

It was in 1933 when passing down Seventh Avenue in Mount Vernon that he saw Lydia sitting on the bench in front of the store. After a brief romance, they were married at the Parkway Casino in Tuckahoe, New York. He continued doing what he knew, being a junk man along with selling produce in the summer months. Joe, who was Rosie's second husband and head bricklayer foreman for a very large company, offered him a job in 1948 as a scaffold man and laborer. Jimmy who was never afraid of hard work, accepted. The pay was really good, but you had to have, as the saying went, "A back of iron." Putting up and taking down scaffold in the fifties was a very dangerous job. They were built of wood nailed together, and the work was done mostly on high-rise buildings. Joe gave jobs to many men in the family. However, only Jimmy and his son-in-law Chuck were able to stick it out.

Jimmy worked for the company over twenty years until his body just couldn't do it anymore. He wasn't a person that showed his emotions to people, even his children. He did it with deeds. I remember him quite often, giving my mother a hug from behind when she was washing dishes. She would say, "Jimmy, the children." Other than that, he didn't show much outward emotion.

In the early fifties, my sister, Joyce, had an eye operation. Every morning, he would go up to her room in the hospital to see how she was feeling, sneaking past the nurses before he went to work. In the evening, on his way home, he would park his car on the side of the hospital where her room was and call up to her.

When my girl cousins got married and set up house, my dad, who loved clamming, would go to Mamaroneck and, in low water with his rake, pick clams and put them in a basket. He would bring them home, open them, and then cook them with linguine. Dad would bring them to his nieces' houses. How they used to talk to me about their Uncle Jimmy with such fondness and love.

In 1960, I'd joined the army and was in boot camp at Fort Dix in New Jersey. On a Friday, while crawling under barbed wire with live ammunition, a fellow soldier panicked, stood up, and was killed. It was reported on TV; however, the person's name wasn't released. The news said it was at Fort Dix, and nothing else was released to the public. That Sunday morning, I was getting dressed in my barracks.

A fellow soldier called out to me, "DeFillippo, your father is here."

Rushing out hoping nothing had happened to anyone in my family, there was Dad with a big smile on his face.

He said, "How are you doing? Want to go to church?" which we did! After Mass, he told me my mom was worried when she heard what happened to a fellow soldier. He then called her on the phone and said, "Someone wants to talk to you." When I got on the phone, my mom started to cry. She then told me that when she woke up, my dad was gone and hadn't known where he went, not knowing anything about him coming to Fort Dix which was a two-hour drive from our home. That day at age twenty-two,

I realized that my father loved me. In those days, Italian American men very seldom expressed to their children, especially the boys, their love for them. It was done by all the deeds they did, not by words. In 1964, Dad was diagnosed with kidney disease. There was no talk about dialysis or transplants in those days. His health continued to decline. He never complained but just took it as it was, even after having heart failure and then leukemia, which took his life on September 9, 1968, at the young age of fifty-seven. My main regret was that I never told him I loved him and thanked him for always providing for his family, doing whatever it took.

Cristina and her sister Molly at her daughter
Lydia's wedding to "Fat" Jimmy—1933

Jimmy DeFillippo with Joyce and Neil in front of the Store with Grandma Cristina Covino in the background—1941

Two of Rose's children, Tina and Alfonso (Sonny) as flower girl and ring bearer at their Aunt Lydia and Uncle Jimmy's wedding at the elaborate Parkway Casino in Tuckahoe, New York—September 6, 1933.

CHAPTER 11

The Other Fred

BESIDES CRISTINA'S BROTHER Fred, there was another Fred in the family. It was her first cousin that was born to her father's sister. They were both named after their grandfather. Cristina's children and grandchildren called him uncle out of respect for an older cousin. He was the same age as Cristina, and they were very close to one another growing up in Italy. Fred and his family migrated to America in 1915 and had settled in New Jersey. He was twenty-seven. He worked in Italian restaurants, starting as a busboy, then as a waiter, and finally becoming manager of an upscale restaurant. With his Italian accent and handsome appearance, he made quite a compliment to the restaurant that he managed. He had never married and visited Cristina at the store quite often. At the age of thirty-eight, he met and fell in love with a woman from the neighborhood where he had lived in New Jersey. The only problem was, she was already married. Her husband, who was known to have a violent temper, found out about the affair, and let it be known that when he found Fred, he would kill him! Fred learned of the threat!

One night after he closed the restaurant where he worked, the woman's husband approached Fred and pulled out a large knife. Fred reached out asking the person to not use the knife. As the man continued to come at him, Fred reached into his jacket, pulled out a gun, and shot and killed the man. He then ran from the scene and, two days later, left for California. In those days, when an Italian killed someone, it was almost never considered justified.

Fred couldn't take a chance to notify his family of how he was doing because they were being watched by law enforcement. However, the law enforcers had no idea of the cousin living in Mount Vernon, New York. Fred wrote Cristina quite often. His sisters and brothers would go to Brooklyn where Cristina's sister Amelia (Molly) lived. The reason for their visit was to get the letters from Fred brought to Brooklyn by the Covino family.

In 1931, after living for five years in California, Fred returned to New Jersey. He surrendered to the police and was put under arrest. The family hired the top lawyer they could find. However, he was very expensive, so Cristina gave the family some money to help pay for Fred's defense. In 1933, he was found guilty of manslaughter, not the first-degree murder he was originally charged with. He received a sentence of twelve to fifteen years in prison. The prison in reality was a farm-type institution. I remember going to visit him with my family in 1945 before his release.

He was pleasant and took us into a store at the prison and bought us a lamp in the shape of a camel, that we had for many years. The woman, whose husband he killed, visited him quite often. He was released in 1945 and married her. Cristina was one of the few people invited to the wedding. The couple were happily married until Fred's passing at the age of eighty-seven.

CHAPTER 12

World War II—All In

1941–1945

ON A SUNDAY morning in Hawaii while most people were sleeping, the Japanese made an all-out aerial attack, catching most of America's naval ships docked with their sailors sleeping in the port at Pearl Harbor. The destruction was immense, killing almost three thousand people and crippling most of the ships. With this and the fact that America was already leaning to join the fight in Europe, it declared an all-out war against the "Axis of Evil" that included Japan, Germany, and Italy. America and its people were all in, creating the greatest war machine the world had ever seen.

Cristina's nephews and cousins joined the armed services as did the people from all over the country. Many of those from Italian American families at the beginning of the war were sent to Europe, with Northern Africa and Southern Italy being their predominant drop-off spot. This was because most of them were first-generation Americans and spoke Italian fluently. In 1942, with the war taking a great toll on Italian economy and its war machine, Benito Mussolini, Italy's leader, appealed to Italian Americans through channels to send money, jewelry, and anything of value to Italy. Some of Cristina's friends still had an underlying love for their home country and their many relatives that were still there. They did in fact contribute to some degree. Also, there was pressure put on Cristina to contribute to Italy. Her reply was "This is the country, America, where my children, nephews, and nieces were born, where they have received wonderful educations, where their possibilities in life have no limit, where I have prospered." Her final words were "Ma tu sei pazzo." (You are crazy.) No way.

During the latter part of the war, Fat Jimmy's car had blackout shades on the windows. Whenever he was driving and an air-raid siren sounded, he would pull over, shut off the lights, and would bring the shades down over the windows. Also, when the sirens went off and you were in your house, the air-raid wardens who were assigned to your block would go up and down the street, yelling at people to put out their lights. Rose, Lydia's sister, was working in a defense plant which, before the war, was an auto plant and was turned into making tanks. The plant wasn't far from where Lydia and her family lived. Rose worked the night shift at the plant which went twenty-four hours a day. When she got off work, she went to their house to get some sleep. Fat Jimmy worked in the Brooklyn Navy Yard and Todd's Shipyard as a machinist where they made ships for the war effort. Everyone was committed in some way to the effort.

Fat Jimmy's three brothers, who were younger, all went into the service and were sent to the Pacific theater to battle the Japanese. Joe was a medic in an elite group called Merrill's Marauders. They went through Burma, which was occupied by the Japanese, causing mayhem for them. On one such mission, Merrill broke his troops into two groups who were to go in different directions to meet at the same point. Joe's group was ambushed by the Japanese, and most were killed. He and other soldiers that survived were able to escape into the jungle, surviving on whatever food they could find. Many of them came down with various diseases. After missing for quite a while, his family was informed that Joe was MIA and probably dead. Fat Jimmy's family were grief-stricken. A short while after, however, they received a letter saying he was found alive. Fat Jimmy received a phone call from his sister Mary telling him the good news. They had been found by allies that were out on patrol.

I remember Uncle Joe coming to the store to see my dad and mom. He was very thin and was shaking and sweating. My mom told me he had picked up several diseases while in Burma, including Malaria. Joe had his picture in the local paper with the story about him, calling him a hero— something he never called himself. He received the Purple Heart for being wounded and the Bronze Star. That was for crawling to a wounded comrade whose guts were literally hanging out of his body. Joe shoved the guts back into the soldier's body, taped it with large bandages, and dragged him back to American lines. The soldier was sent to an evacuation hospital and, after hours of surgery, survived.

After many years of living in Mount Vernon with his family, they moved to Florida. Healthwise, he never became 100 percent, and as he got older, his health continued to worsen. The Department of Defense gave him a special car and put a swimming pool where he lived.

Another hero from the family was Fat Jimmy's nephew Arnold Peluso. He was, even as a teenager, hell-bent to create mayhem. Living in Mount Vernon and with his dad having a junkyard one block from the store, he quite often would drive his motorcycle up on the sidewalk of Cristina's business. She would come out of the store and yell at him in Italian to get off the sidewalk, which, out of respect, he always did. Arnold joined the navy and served in the Atlantic Ocean in the European theater. The ship he was on was torpedoed, and he jumped into the ocean to survive. Being an excellent swimmer, he managed to survive until he, along with others some of whom he managed to help keep afloat, were rescued by an American ship. He was put into a hospital in South Hampton, England, where he met and married a British girl named Iris.

They returned to Mount Vernon, and Arnold joined his father in the junk business. His father had bought a home in Pelham, New York, where the family had moved to. After a few years, the home and property were bought by the government to build a portion of a thruway. His father sold the business; and the family, including Arnold, his wife, and children moved to Florida. Arnold joined Jimmy Hoffa in organizing the labor unions across Florida. By the

1960s, he had become the union president of local 787 of the laborers' Union-AFL-CIO of Palm Beach County. By that time, he and his wife, Iris, had become estranged. He was living in a studio apartment and had stated more than once to the family that he felt his life was in danger. He would always look through the blinds to see who was at his door when his bell would ring or when there was a knock. Shots rang out at his apartment on the evening of July 22, 1968. His neighbor called the police. When they entered Arnold's apartment, they found Arnold shot to death. His family felt a woman must have been involved one way or another as this was his weak point. So here was a man who was born in 1925, joined the Navy, was a hero in the Second World War, and shot dead at the young age of forty-three.

On the opposite side of the scale, there was a man who many in the family felt was a coward. One of the families that came to the store quite often had a son-in-law who came from Italy and married their only daughter in a family with many sons. In 1945, he was drafted to go into the army; however, he was afraid of possibly going into combat. On a Sunday while at the store for a delicious meal, he conspired with some of the other men there to get him drunk and break his arm so that when he had to go for induction at Whitehall Street, Manhattan, he would be rejected. Sure enough after much wine, the men took him to the basement and did what he had asked them to. Lydia said you could hear the screams coming from the basement as his arm was broken. When he went to be inducted, he was given a temporary deferment and told to come back in eight weeks. When he did go back and was expecting to get a permanent deferment, to his surprise, he was found to be fit for duty immediately. So there you are—two men who were heroes, another who was a coward. This played out many times in many families across the land.

In 1943, Cristina made her third real-estate investment in a multifamily home at 359 South Fifth Avenue, two blocks from the store. In 1947, Rose moved into this home and finally had a place to settle into. Over the years, many family members lived in the other apartments in the home, paying low rent so they could save for the future. This was just one of many ways that Cristina helped her family.

In 1945, the war ended. President Truman had told Japan to surrender, which they refused to do. Fearing the loss of possibly over one million allied forces in an invasion of Japan, he decided to drop bombs that had been developed that would have catastrophic results. The first was dropped on the city of Hiroshima; however, the Japanese government still refused to surrender. After that, a second bomb was dropped on Nagasaki. Finally, the Japanese surrendered. This type of bomb had been developed by what came to be known as the "Manhattan Project." The bomb was called the atom bomb, which is still today the most lethal weapon ever known to man.

Germany had surrendered in Europe when their leader, Adolf Hitler, and his mistress, Eva Braun, who he had married just a few weeks before, committed suicide as the Russian army closed in on their bunker. Mussolini had set up a rouge government in 1943 when Italy formally surrendered. This was done with the German government helping him to escape from prison. In 1945, he was located in Lake Como by the partisans, was badly beaten, and then hung. The Italian troops fought poorly in North Africa and Southern Italy, bringing their part in the war to an early surrender because their hearts weren't in it. The cousins had told the family what poor fighters the Italian troops were at the time. However, the partisans were, in many cases, heroes as they helped fight the Germans for the next two years.

Cristina's nephews from Brooklyn, who fought in the Second World War and returned home, began to get married. The family would go to Brooklyn to attend what were called "football weddings." It was named that way because it consisted of beer, wine, soda, and sandwiches called "heroes." They had labels on them indicating what was inside and were placed on the table. If there were some that no one wanted, we would trade them with another table by throwing them to that table in exchange for something on the table that we liked. Thus, the name "football weddings"! All the family, including the children, were invited as the weddings weren't very expensive but were unbelievably full of fun.

In the late forties, the Sunday dinners at Cristina's continued. There was a piano in the dining room part of the kitchen that Uncle Fred and Aunt Olga both played. Many of the guests brought along their instruments; and after dinner, they would start to play while drinking wine, eating fruits and nuts. Each grandchild would go up to the piano with Cristina standing behind and telling them the Italian words, which they would sing out as best they could.

The grown-ups would laugh because as we found out years later, the songs were often off-colored to say the least. By far, the best singer among us was my cousin Jerry, Aunt Fannie and Uncle Copey's son. My aunt Fannie, as I stated earlier, had a beautiful voice, and Uncle Copey could also sing well. So it was no wonder that, at such a young age, he was the singing star in the family. Later in life, Jerry had a very successful singing career. His family's last name was Vitaliano, which Jerry had legally changed.

Cristina (2nd from left) attending a wedding with her daughter's Fannie (far left) and Rose (far right) and her son Nick—late 1940s.

Arnold Peluso, WW II Hero, shot dead at the age of 43—1964

CHAPTER 13

Vitaliano to Vale

BEING EIGHT YEARS older than me, my first recollection of my cousin Jerry was when I was about six years old. We had a coal furnace in the basement of our home, and I would go down and watch him shovel in the coal. We had pigeons in the backyard of the house as this was Uncle Skinny Jimmy's favorite pastime. Jerry had developed a love for pigeons as I had. Jerry made money shining shoes at the local barbershop, singing while he worked. As a teenager, he would sing at amateur nights at the local movie theaters throughout Westchester County and the Bronx. Our family would pack the theater and clap, whistle, scream—whatever it took to make him win. As I can best remember, he won every time, not because of our cheering, but because he was just the best. His signature song was "Prisoner of Love," which was a big recording hit for Perry Como. Jerry became friendly with Perry later in life and said he was such a nice, unassuming person even though he was a megastar. Jerry left high school before graduating as the only thing on his mind was singing. His father had other ideas because he had quit school! He brought him to work with him in construction. Jerry's very easy job was to oil his father's steam shovel in the morning and again at lunch. Other than that, he just sat around until it was time to go home. For this he got paid very well as it was a union job. However, he quit because singing was in his soul, and that was all he wanted to do. He got jobs singing at local entertainment clubs in Westchester and the Bronx.

Jerry got his first break while singing at a club in Yonkers, New York. Guy Mitchell, who was a prominent singer at the time, did a one-night stand at the club that Jerry was working at. When Mitchell heard him singing before he went on as the prime entertainer, Mitchell was very impressed with Jerry's voice, so much so that he got Mitch Miller, the headman at Columbia Records, to give Jerry an audition. Upon watching and listening to the audition, Miller signed him to a contract. His first hit, "Two Purple Shadows on the Snow," in the early fifties got his career off and running. He was making a good living singing at clubs up and down the East Coast. He was kept in the area by his manager at the time who lived in New York and preferred to be close to home.

The wise guys in Rhode Island and Boston loved his voice and got him all the work he wanted in clubs they either owned or at least had control over. One such club was "The Frolic" in Rhode Island. While Jerry was appearing there, he saw an ad for another local club, which showed a picture of the star performing by the name of

Rita Grabel. He thought she was beautiful, and being a single young man, he asked a friend of his that knew her to ask if they could go for coffee after they both finished their performances that night. Her response was a yes; and from that time on, Jerry's career and love for Rita became the two most important things in his life, definitely with Rita being the most important. She loved him very much to the point of giving up her own ambitions to concentrate after they married on his career and their children. The range in Jerry's voice "was second to none." All you have to do is listen to him sing "Sorrento," "And This is My Beloved," and "Enchanted," just to name a few, and you would see he needed not take a back seat to any singer.

Rita knew Jerry would be accepted by the entire nation, not just the East Coast. While living in New Jersey, he got out of the contract with his then manager. One night while appearing at the Copacabana in New York, Frank Sinatra came in to watch the show. Being impressed with Jerry's performance, he asked him to go to Las Vegas and appear at the Sands, which Frank owned points in. Jerry and Rita decided it would be a good career move. He started in the lounge, where he was doing standing-room-only business. One night when Jerry Lewis, who was scheduled to appear in the main room took ill, management asked Vale to replace him. His show was met with much praise by the local newspapers and much applause from the audience.

He caught the eye of Howard Hughes who offered him a contract to sing in Las Vegas only at his hotel, the Frontier. In those days in Vegas, the entertainers appeared five or six days a week and were paid very well. He and

Rita decided the contract was too lucrative to pass on. So they packed up the family; and these two East Coast people, Rita was from Brooklyn, went west. They bought a home in Las Vegas, surrounded in the neighborhood by fellow entertainers, such as Totie Fields, Sergio Franchi, Bob Newhart, and Pat Cooper who Jerry years later had a falling-out with due to Pat Cooper's jealousy.

Rita will always be loved by our family. Whenever we see or talk to her, she makes every one of us seem special. Jerry suffered and survived a severe stroke in 2002. At this point, she became more protective of her husband than ever before. Despite what Rita did to help him recover, he continued to decline. Twelve years after his stroke, on May 14, 2014, he passed away at his home in Palm Desert, California, at the age of eighty-three. To my cousin Jerry, thank you for making me proud, and as Bob Hope used to say, "Thanks for the memories." I will treasure them forever.

Jerry Vale singing for his 1st performance at Carnegie Hall—1963

CHAPTER 14

Wine, Peaches, and Glen Island Beach

NEVER REMEMBER DINNER being served without wine on the table at Grandma's. Whether it was family or family and friends, wine was a staple. Uncle Fred was the master wine-maker. From when he got the grapes in crates that grandma had bought, which were only the finest, he dedicated himself to his passion making the "wine fit for kings" as he used to say. He had part of the cellar floor dug down two steps in the coolest part of the store basement, built a cement shelf, then put a door which became the wine cellar. Uncle Fred made four barrels of burgundy red wine each season. To say it was hearty but delicious was an understatement.

In some of the pitchers that were put on the table with wine in them, very large dry peaches were added, which absorbed the wine. These special peaches were available from the end of October until January. They couldn't be found in every store. My grandmother would have one of her sons-in-laws drive her to Arthur Avenue in the Bronx, where they were available. She would buy them by the box. The peaches were cut into pieces then put in the wine. They weren't just for the adults! When the babies would cry, the mothers would put a piece of peach on their lips and let them suck on it. After a very short while, the babies would stop crying and go to sleep. Even the children who were no longer babies would get a piece of peach to eat, sometimes two or three. This would take the pepper out of their assess when it started to get late.

In the summer, Grandma and Uncle Fred would take the younger grandchildren to Glen Island Beach in New Rochelle, New York. She would pack cardboard boxes with macaroni, gravy, meat, desserts, Italian bread, salad, and Pepsi-Cola. Uncle Fred would also bring a gallon of his wine. The park would close at 8:00 p.m., except for our family. The police would let us stay and come by our table where there was always food waiting for them, along with a small glass of "Uncle Fred's Red." They were all great guys, even playing ball with the kids and singing along as Uncle Fred played his banjo, which he had also mastered. These were the best of times my sister Joyce and I still remember seventy-five years later with such fondness.

CHAPTER 15

Television and Real Estate in the 1940s

IN 1948, OUR neighbors on Seton Avenue, which was the house Grandma had bought during the Depression, Phil and Minnie Rella, bought the first TV on our block. It was a seven-and-a-half-inch Philco. It was put on a table in the unfinished basement of the home. They allowed us to come in and watch it with their son Carlo. They would put a green filter on it to cut down on the glare, and to some extent, it produced a color.

In 1949, Dad and Mom bought our first TV. A twelve-and-a-half-inch DuMont with a cabinet, which in those days was a big deal. It was to arrive in October on what was the first day of the World Series between the New York Yankees and the Brooklyn Dodgers. My mom let me stay home from school that day, which she never did unless I had a fever. Between 12:00 and 12:30 p.m., the men arrived and installed the TV. At 1:00 p.m., the game started. It was a fantastic pitching duel between Allie

Reynolds for the Yankees, who was part Native American, and Don Newcome who was Black. I mention this because it was only two years after Major League Baseball had, in 1947, signed Jackie Robinson as the first Black to play in the major leagues, which was a historic event not only in sports but also had a tremendous meaning for the United States. The score was 0–0, going into the bottom of the ninth inning when Tommy Henrich, known as Old Reliable, hit a home run for the Yankees, and they won 1–0. Both pitchers pitched the whole nine innings, which you will never see today. That day, my mother became a Yankee fan and continued to be until she passed away at the age of almost 101.

Having the taste of real estate already on her tongue with her purchases up to that point and with the war over, in 1946, Grandma Cristina bought two lots next to the store, which she kept as lots for many years to give her privacy to conduct business.

In 1947, she bought a three-family home on Fifth Street in Mount Vernon between Fourth and Fifth Avenues. The price of the home was $3,100. It, at the end, didn't benefit the Covino family. Uncle Fred in 1949 fell in love with a woman who was from his hometown in Italy and, with her two sons, had come to America in 1948. Grandma was told by some of her friends in America that the woman had a checkered past. Grandma wrote her family in Italy, inquiring about this woman. Her family wrote back saying the woman indeed was not well thought of. She had buried three husbands over the years and had sold all their properties. She had come under investigation by the police for the way they had died. Before any further investigation could take place, she left for America. Grandma confronted Uncle Fred with what she had been told, going as far as showing him the letters from his two sisters still living in Italy. He told her he didn't care what they wrote. He loved her and wanted to get married. He had made up his mind. Grandma not only gave them a wedding but signed over the house on Fourth Street to him as a wedding gift. However, she took him out of her will wherein he would have shared in the rest of the estate. She told him it was because she didn't trust his wife. After he told his wife what Grandma had said, she forbade him from going to the store and being with his family. Less than three years after they were married, he passed away. My mother and aunts were sure in their minds his wife had done something to hasten his death. Before they could have the police investigate it, she sold the house and moved back to Italy. However, not to the original town she came from as the DiPalo family, who lived in the town, was waiting for her to serve what they felt was justice.

Grandma needed help at the store as Uncle Fred had gone to live with his wife and her two children in the house she had given him. Aunt Olga and Uncle Jimmy, as they didn't have any children, agreed to live with her. Aunt Olga, a very intelligent person, was a plus to the business almost immediately. She told the number players that if they brought in numbers from other people, she would give them 25 percent off their own bets. The people that did that were called runners. She would also give her big runners free packs of cigarettes or bottles of soda or candy.

For Christmas, she ordered cases of excellent liquor and gave them out to all the big players. This was done after Grandma okayed it.

Aunt Olga felt that any future real-estate transactions should be to buy homes on the north side of Mount Vernon. The homes were larger and more expensive. However, the rents were much better. On September 6, 1950, Grandma made her first real-estate venture into the north side. Most of these homes were built from the late 1800s to the 1920s as one family homes. They had maid quarters on the third floor, which could be converted into an apartment. The second floor, where the bedrooms were, also got converted into an apartment, as well as the first floor that had been where the kitchen, living room, dining room, and, in some cases, library were. When the stock market crashed, these homeowners who were, in many cases, doctors, lawyers, bankers, and stockbrokers were practically ruined financially, and thus the conversion so as not to lose their homes. Some who were not able to get the finances for these conversions walked away from them, and then those who bought them made the conversions. The home that was bought was at 137 North Primrose Avenue. Grandma bought it for $14,500. She bought a home at 225 North Fulton Avenue also for $14,500. In 1954, she bought another home at 135 Wallace Avenue for $11,000. The lower price was because the home needed extensive repair. Grandma knew that her friends, many of whom were in construction, would love to have interior work to do in the winter. With their excellent workmanship, it turned out to be a beautiful home.

So here was this immigrant woman who, at age sixteen, arrived in America in 1904; became by 1954 the owner of seven multifamily homes, empty lots, and stocks in some of the largest companies; and through her grit and hard work, had achieved the American dream and beyond!

CHAPTER 16

Gambling and More Gambling

By THE EARLY 1950s, Mount Vernon became an open city, as far as gambling was concerned. Grandma stayed with what she knew best: alcohol and numbers. She stayed away from sports betting and horses. To give you an idea of how many gambling parlors there were, starting on Mundy Lane, which was on the Bronx border, to Fifth Avenue, all of which were on Sandford Boulevard, there was a bar, candy store, another candy store where my friends and I would go to have milkshakes, a gas station, my grandmother's store on Seventh Avenue and a store on Fifth Avenue. This was within only eight blocks. They all carried on legal business as well, not to mention other places throughout Mount Vernon run by American-born men. There were none that were run better than how this immigrant woman ran hers. It was a tight, unassuming, well-oiled machine.

Some of the places made more money than the store; but Grandma had exceptionally loyal customers, most of whom were Black Americans. They remembered all she had done for them when times were hard and, above all, trusted her. In fact, all of them had paid back whatever was in the "book."

As a counterpoint, distant relatives whom Grandma had loaned money to during the Depression so they wouldn't lose their homes never repaid the loan after they started doing well. Grandma never asked for the money back. She felt they knew what she had done for them, and it would be on their conscience for the rest of their lives.

As far as the local bookies went, most of them had a problem that my grandmother never had. That was, they were gamblers themselves. In the evening, they would go to Yonkers Raceway, which was just minutes away, dine in the restaurant, and bet large amounts of money on the horses. On weekends, some of them would go to the private crap and card games. They were called "floating crap games" as each week, the locations changed. People would, in many instances, rent out their basements to those running the game. There were not only bookies at the game! Many of the players were doctors, lawyers, and wealthy types that loved the action and also betting alongside the people from the underworld.

Everyone was picked up at preordained locations and brought to the game. When they arrived, they were greeted by girls offering free drinks and food. Those that ran the game made their money by taking a share of the betting and being the house, as it would be in the casinos. While these habits were most of the bookies' Achilles' heel, Grandma's passion was real estate. This turned out to be the much better option.

Some of them would come to her to borrow money so they could pay off on hits as they had tapped out at the race track the night before, always paying her back with thanks in the form of money beyond what she had loaned them.

Though she was in the gambling business, she on many occasions would express to us her desire that we didn't gamble, especially betting on horse racing where she used to tell us, "You can't beat the horses. They have four legs and you only have two."

CHAPTER 17

Work for It!

GRANDMA DID NOT like giving her money to anyone unless there was a very good reason, even to her grandchildren, who she made feel they had to do something to earn it. The one exception was at Christmas. She would give us five dollars each, reaching into her apron that she always wore and taking out rolls of bills that were tied together by a rubber band. She would wait for us to kiss her, then gave us the money and said in what we call broken English, "Merry Christmas. Grandma loves you." Those words meant so much to me and still does to this day. The rest of the year, she would give us chores to do to receive any extra money.

On Saturdays, during the tomato-bottling season, the grandchildren would gather around the kitchen table at the store and received one cent for each bottle we filled. When lunchtime came, she gave us cold-cut sandwiches and a bottle of Pepsi. Speaking of Pepsi, Grandma saw the advantages of selling it. She felt the taste was as good as

Coke, and with Pepsi, you got twice as much for the same price. Her customers loved the idea of "twice as much for the same price" and asked for it instead of Coke. In fact, there was a jingle out at that time which went, "Pepsi-Cola hits the spot. Twelve full ounces, that's a lot. Twice as much for a nickel too. Pepsi-Cola is the drink for you." At that time, she made her last trip to Wall Street and bought, you guessed it, stock in Pepsi. What an amazing person, who was sharp as a tack when it came to business.

After lunch, we went back to bottling tomatoes until 3:00 p.m. Another example of pay for work, my sister, Joyce, and Aunt Rosie's Tina would go to the houses Grandma owned on Saturdays and cleaned the hallways and stairs. They would get fifty cents apiece for each house. Whenever she would let us have a box of cookies, it would be after we cleaned the floor in the store and on the sidewalk outside. What a learning experience for all of us: nothing comes free. Speaking of my sister, Joyce, I remember as little children going to the doctor's office to have our tonsils taken out. After the operation, I was fine; Joyce, not so good. In those days, one of the healing tools was to eat something very cold. Grandma sent two gallons of ice cream to us by Uncle Fred. I ate mine with delight. My sister, however, was vomiting and couldn't eat hers, so I was forced (*ha ha*) to eat it. From being a small child until I was about ten, whenever I was at the store, Grandma would take me into the kitchen and make me an eggnog, which consisted of raw eggs, milk, a spoon of chocolate powder, and a small glass of sweet vermouth. Boy, did I love those eggnogs.

When it came to immediate family, whenever any of them went to her for financial help, she didn't hesitate to delve deeply into why they were put into such a position. Was it caused by their own missteps or was it things beyond their control? She didn't hesitate to ask many questions; if they didn't like being asked things, most of the time she would deny their request. Cristina would make it clear the money was a loan, not a gift. Never charging interest, she would ask how they were going to repay her. When they told her how, she would expect them to live up to their obligation. She had it all put down in writing. If anyone didn't want to sign, she would not follow through on the loan, as she felt that they couldn't be trusted. In many cases, Cristina forgave the loan if those borrowing money were living up to their obligation to repay.

CHAPTER 18

Those Wonderful Fifties Until…

IN THE EARLY fifties, Grandma sold one of the lots farthest from the store to a church. The rest of the lots remained patrolled by dogs on long chains. She had dogs as far back as I could remember. They slept outside in doghouses that different people in the family had built. I don't remember any of them ever being allowed in the house. They ate leftovers from what Grandma, Uncle Jimmy, and Aunt Olga didn't finish. Their diet consisted of macaroni (I never heard of pasta until I was in my twenties), wet bread, meat bones, and chicken bones, which they crushed with their teeth before swallowing them. I don't remember any of them choking to death on the bones. They were after all animals, not these cutesy dogs that you see around today. You couldn't go near them unless accompanied by Grandma or Uncle Jimmy. Then the dogs would be very relaxed. I think they were bilingual because she would yell at them in Italian, and Uncle Jimmy yelled in English. And the dogs would understand both of them. In the fifties, Grandma started selling dog food in the store. She tried giving it to her dogs, but they would smell it and refuse to eat it. She went back to feeding them scraps from the table, which they couldn't get enough of.

In the summers when Grandma went to Italy, our family would go to the store on Sundays so my mom could help Aunt Olga. She also went by herself during the week as it was only four blocks from where we lived. Aunt Rosie also did the same.

On Sundays, we would often go across the street into a small white church where the congregation was entirely Black. We, which included my sister, Joyce, and my cousins, would sit in the back and watch the parishioners pray. What we liked best was when they sang. Here were these lovely people all dressed in white singing out with such joy in their hearts. The pastor was a big man and had the help of his sons. He would have a smile on his face and would welcome us warmly. After the Mass, which lasted for hours, the parishioners would go across the street to the store and buy ice cream, soda, and anything else that would cool them off. At 2:00 p.m., the store closed, and our families sat down to dinner. After dinner, we would talk for a while, and then the men would go down to the basement and play cards. Most of the time, the game was knock rummy.

Uncle Joe, Aunt Rose's husband, Fat and Skinny Jimmy, and my cousin Tina's husband, George, usually played until about 9:00 p.m., when the game would break up as the men had to go to work the next day. Uncle Joe some years later ran into a serious problem with the law.

He was, however, a welcome addition to our family as Aunt Rose had divorced Harry the Horse. Uncle Joe was always smiling and generous to a fault.

While the men were playing cards, the children would walk to the Embassy Theater, which was fourteen blocks from the store. The reason they walked so far was because Aunt Rosie worked as a cashier at the theater during the week and her daughter Rita, the oldest cousin, was the cashier on the weekend. All the children, which usually was about six of them, were allowed in for free.

CHAPTER 19

Uncle Joe—Big Time

AUNT ROSIE'S SECOND husband, Joe, was a good man as I mentioned earlier. We all have weaknesses; his was young women. After he and Aunt Rosie were married for quite a few years, he started to fool around. Young women can be very expensive when you yourself aren't that young anymore. Although he made excellent money, there just wasn't enough to support his lifestyle. In construction, there were shop stewards who were put there by the unions. They were supposed to work and look out for the men. Very few of them did any work but were paid their salaries every week. In reality, it was the payoff by the construction companies to keep peace on the job and to not have any problems with the men.

Most of these shop stewards were connected, in one way or another, to the Mafia. Uncle Joe had dealings with them on the job. After a while, he started hanging with them after work. Wherever these guys hung out was where the "hot" girls were. He spread his money around these bars to be a show-off to the young girls. He was approached by these supposed friends and asked if he wanted to make some easy money. All he had to do was drop off a package to Upstate New York. Nelson Rockefeller was the governor of New York from 1959 to 1973. When he first came into office, he had a liberal drug attitude and policy. However, this failed miserably, and heroin drug use had become rampant. The people of the state were up in arms and wanted something done. Rockefeller changed his policy and went to the other extreme, making it a law that anyone arrested with more than a certain amount of heroin for sale, if convicted, would receive a life sentence without any chance for parole or plea bargaining.

One night in the early sixties, Uncle Joe had decided to make the fast easy big money and traveled to Upstate New York. He was stopped by New York state troopers who found the package which contained heroin and was arrested. He was convicted of trying to distribute a large amount of heroin. Here was a man who was afraid to even get a traffic ticket. He was sentenced as the law required to life without parole. He suffered a heart attack while in prison, but he recovered. He was a model prisoner and taught many prisoners the bricklaying trade.

Sometime later, I attended a funeral for a friend who passed away at a very young age from a form of cancer. His brother-in-law by the name of Tony, who had been a good friend of mine as we grew up, was at the funeral. We hugged as we hadn't seen each other for a long time. Although I had written him while he was in prison at Lewisburg,

Pennsylvania, and he wrote back. He had become a made member of the Mafia. As we talked, somehow I brought up my Uncle Joe who had gotten the life sentence.

My friend said to me, "That's your Uncle?"

When I replied, "Yes, he was married to my mother's sister."

He first asked how my mom was, then he said, "We called him Pop! He was set up because someone had to take a fall to make it look like Rockefeller's law was having some effect."

I was, to say the least, surprised, but I didn't say anything to anyone as my friend told me this in confidence. Hugh Carey became governor from January 1, 1975, to 1983. When he was leaving office, he gave out pardons to different people. Uncle Joe was one of those pardoned.

He lived the rest of his life as a model citizen. Aunt Rose and he had divorced before he was in any trouble. I saw him from time to time as he lived close to a business that I owned after he got out of prison. He had served twenty-three years in prison, but we still had a good relationship even after all those years.

He didn't smile as much like he did in the old days and was very limited in making conversations. All this I understood as I found it to be the same with anyone who served time. We never talked about the old days when he was married to Aunt Rose. Uncle Joe didn't talk about his time in prison and what put him there, and I never asked. I did, however, remember him as one who gave my father a job and was always so generous to me with extra money and by being very kind.

CHAPTER 20

No More Liquor, Much More Numbers

IN 1951, THE store was again raided by the Feds. Although prohibition was long over, Grandma was still selling alcohol without a tax stamp. I remember sitting on the green bench in front of the store, which had been repainted so many times. It was a Sunday afternoon when two cars pulled up in front and Feds jumped out. They tried to get in the door, but it was locked. They got sledgehammers and tried to break the door down to no avail as it was now made of heavy steel. When my mom and aunts had disposed of any liquor that was around, they calmly let the Feds in. Not finding any liquor, they arrested Grandma anyway because they had a witness ready to testify that he bought liquor from her. She was put in the paddy wagon that had pulled up after the two cars with law enforcement agents in them. Off they drove with my little grandmother in it. I was devastated!

I ran inside and heard my aunt Olga tell my mother to call Wolf. That was Wolf Cribari, the family's lawyer. I never knew his real first name. He was called Wolf because whenever he was in court handling a case, he was ruthless and cunning. He went to the federal building and got her out on bail. She was able to sleep in her own bed by Monday evening. After paying a fine, Grandma was released by a judge two weeks later. This was however her second offense. Aunt Rose had two pinches by Mount Vernon Police for numbers. They let her take the arrests instead of Grandma. Aunt Olga had one, and my mom none. Aunt Fannie, raising her family, wasn't involved in the day-to-day goings-on at the store. Back in those days, there was something called a "three-time loser." I am not sure exactly how it worked, but no one wanted to become one. It seemed that anyone with three felonies could go away for a very long time.

When Grandma returned from Italy that fall, the three daughters told her it was time to stop selling liquor. As the number business was thriving, she agreed. Aunt Olga was constantly improving the business. She started taking what was called the "lead." It was betting on the first number that came out in the day's number. The payout was eight to one.

Each year, Grandma continued going to Italy in May and returning in September. She, for the next four years, traveled only first class, bringing with her gifts and money for her two sisters that still lived in Italy and other relatives. After her first visit, the relatives would meet her at the ship in large numbers at the port in Naples. She had said numerous times that they didn't care how hard she had worked to become wealthy. They just wanted a piece of the pie!

Aunt Olga said to Grandma (you never told her what to do; you could however suggest) if they offered their steady players 25 percent on any bets they brought in from other people, they could use it against money they had to pay for their own bets. At first, Grandma resisted, thinking that if you gave people honest and friendly service, they would bring in bets from other people and not expect anything in return. After a time, she relented. It turned out to be a good move. Many customers became runners (which meant picking up bets from others). This brought in a sizable amount of new action. Sometimes when I was at the store, a customer would come in with a sizable number of bets. When they were leaving, Grandma would tell me to go behind the counter and get them two packs of cigarettes, or if they wanted, I would give them two Hershey bars. You never went behind the counter unless you were told to. Sometimes people would come in to buy canned vegetables, which were all stacked behind the counter. Grandma would tell us to go behind it and, with a long-handled instrument that had hooks on the end, take from the shelves whatever vegetables they wanted to buy. I have it in my possession still today. It brings back memories whenever I look at it.

Neil DeFillippo with the original "Graber" from the 1930's,
to take down items from high shelves at "The Store"

CHAPTER 21

Trips to Italy Continue and so Does the Food

GRANDMA CONTINUED GOING to Italy in the early fifties. In 1953 when I was taking Italian in high school, I wrote her a letter in Italian while she was in Italy. She wrote me back saying how proud of me she was. She also told me that she showed it to all her relatives.

Each year when she returned, it was time for her to start thinking of preparing for Thanksgiving. My father would take her to Arthur Avenue in the Bronx to do her shopping. Sometimes, my dad would bring me along. She would buy most of what she needed at Tannenbaum's, the only Jewish merchant on Arthur Avenue. The rest were all Italian. But Grandma felt Tannenbaum had the best quality, and because of the large quantity they sold, the prices were very good. Little did I know back then that I would marry a real Arthur Avenue girl. My wife, Camille, whose family owned a large grocery store, Leo's, run by her Uncle Sal and Fimianos meat market, owned by her father. Not only were their businesses on Arthur Avenue, they actually lived behind the stores in a house. About the only thing on the menu that wasn't Italian at Grandma's was the fresh turkey she bought.

Grandma and my aunts did the baking, everything from fruit pies to cheesecake. Before we got to the turkey, we would have salad, macaroni, meatballs, sausage, braciola, and pork skin. Then the turkey would be served with all the trimmings. This was followed by nuts, bowls of fruit, and whatever the women baked with coffee either American or espresso. The dinner usually went from 2:00 p.m. to 8:00 or 9:00 p.m. with a little break in between each course. It was always accompanied by wine and large peaches that were put into it. I recall my cousins, who by now had children of their own, giving them pieces of peaches as we all had gotten when we were small.

Christmas was another wonderful holiday for our family. We had live eels swimming in Grandma's bathtub for several days before Christmas Eve, which was part of the seven fishes we ate as an observance to the birth of Christ. There were plenty of side dishes to go along with the fish. Then at midnight, we switched to meat, sausage being the main course. There were sausage with peppers; sausage bread; and sausage and gravy, not brown gravy but red. The children made heroes of all the different types. Heroes were what we called the small loaves of Italian bread. Grandma would make different types of liquor from her alcohol, adding red and green coloring. Then, there were always at least two bottles of anisette which she also made. This was for the espresso which we called black coffee.

We would then go home to our own houses and open our gifts that our parents had put under the Christmas tree before we left for Grandma's earlier in the evening. Waking up on Christmas Day, it was back to the store, dressed in the new clothes we had received from "Santa." After much hugging and kissing from our large family and exchanging gifts, it was back to where we had left off Christmas Eve—eating!

In 1955, Grandma's sister Molly, who had gone through so much with her in the early years of their lives, was diagnosed with breast cancer and had a radical mastectomy. In 1956, Grandma was making plans to go back to Italy again. Her sister and her husband, Uncle Benny, decided to go along to see the two sisters that were still in Italy. However, my sister, Joyce, had planned to get married in early September, which was when Grandma usually came back.

Grandma was afraid she wouldn't be back in time for the wedding and asked Joyce to change the wedding day, which she did. My sister changed the date to May 6, which was good because Grandma never left for Italy until after Mother's Day. My sister was married at Glen Island Casino in New Rochelle, New York. It was a beautiful place, best known for having big bands play there in the 1930s and 1940s which were carried on national radio stations. The wedding was fabulous, and all the relatives from Brooklyn attended.

When Grandma, Aunt Molly, and Uncle Benny went to the pier on the west side to leave on the *Andrea Doria*, they were accompanied by both their immediate families.

The ship set sail, and it was a very pleasant trip to Italy. The family and friends were at the pier in Naples to greet them. By the middle of July, however, Aunt Molly wasn't feeling well, and she and her husband decided to leave for home early. There was no way her sister was going to let her go home without her. The sisters, who had been through so much together, weren't about to be separated when one of them wasn't feeling well.

The ship that was leaving was the Italian liner *Andrea Doria*, the pride of the fleet. However, as the only available space left on the ship was in tourist, they had to decide whether to wait a few more weeks so they could travel first-class on another liner. The decision was made to leave as quickly as possible. It was so crowded they had to share the room with a young lady by the name of Margaret Carola, whose mother and siblings were in the cabin next door. Grandma and Aunt Molly were in cabin 230, and the young lady's family were in 228. Uncle Benny was in another cabin with men. The *Doria* had its maiden voyage on January 14, 1953. It's captain at the time was Captain Calamai as it was in July 1956. The ship had made fifty successful round trips up to that time. The *Doria* was considered to be the most beautiful ship built after World War II. It was considered unsinkable because of many watertight compartments, not unlike the *Titanic*. It had three swimming pools, many pieces of beautiful tapestries, and art. *Doria* set out from Italy for America on July 17, 1956, after stopping at three ports in the Mediterranean. It would take eleven days to arrive in New York!

Cristina at Joyce's bridal shower with Joyce's
future Mother-In-Law Margaret—1956

Cristina with Joyce on her wedding day—May 6, 1956

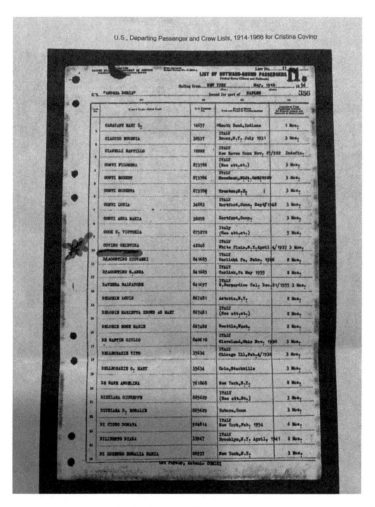

Saturday, May 19, 1956—Cristina Covino named on list of outward-bound passengers, United States of America to Italy on the Andrea Doria

CHAPTER 22

So Close and yet so Far

MOST OF THE trip heading home was very pleasant weather-wise. Aunt Molly was holding up fairly well, except she was tired. On July 25, as *Doria* was approaching the heavily trafficked sea-lanes off Nantucket, Massachusetts, the fog started to roll in. It got heavier and heavier, but the ship had the most modern radar for that time. As night fell, you couldn't see more than ten feet ahead even with bright lights of the *Doria* shining on the water.

The early morning of July 25, a ship with the name of *Stockholm* had left New York bound for Gothenburg, Sweden. It was much smaller than the *Andrea Doria* and, because of its traveling through very frigid waters, had an icebreaker attached to its front.

As evening arrived on the last night, there was much celebration on board. After eating, Aunt Molly wasn't feeling well. She wanted to go down to her cabin. Grandma told Uncle Benny to stay and enjoy himself. She would go with her sister.

As the fog continued to get worse, there was now two junior officers on the bridge with Captain Calamai. The *Andrea Doria* was 53 miles southeast of Nantucket, going almost full speed at 21.8 knots. It was felt by many experts later that he should have been going at a much slower speed, considering the weather. *Stockholm* was heading north of the eastbound lane where, according to maritime law, it should not have been. About 10:45 p.m., Captain Calamai's radar showed a ship which was the *Stockholm*. A few minutes after that, third officer Johan-Ernst Carstens-Johannsen saw the *Doria* on the radar of the *Stockholm*. The two ships came to different conclusions about each other's location. Carstens-Johannsen thought the *Doria* was on the right. Calamai was maneuvering to pass starboard to starboard, which was not a conventional pass, not realizing they were on a collision course until Calamai spotted the lights of the *Stockholm* through the fog. He ordered a hard-left turn to try and outrun the other ship. One of the two other officers on the *Doria*, Bridge, shouted, "She is coming right at us!" Carstens-Johannsen saw the *Doria* and tried to reverse his propellers and slow down; however, it was too late. The *Stockholm*, with the icebreaker on its bow, crashed into the *Doria's* starboard side. It went about thirty feet into the *Doria's* hull. It snapped bulkheads as it penetrated. It was able to break loose, leaving a very large hole in the *Doria*.

CHAPTER 23

Panic, Heroism, and the Darkest of Days

ON IMPACT, THE passengers of the *Andrea Doria* received a very strong jolt and then the loud sound of metal banging. In the lounge, the ship's orchestra was playing "Arrivederci Roma." Suddenly they were hurled from the stage because of the crash. Many people had cuts and bruises. It had a large section on its starboard side turned into twisted metal. After what seemed like an eternity to the passengers and crew on the *Andrea Doria*, which was actually a few minutes at the most, *Stockholm* was put in reverse and backed away. However, the damage had been done; and there was a gaping hole in the side of the *Doria*, which allowed it to fill up with water.

One of the people on board was a teenager by the name of Linda Morgan whose stepfather and stepsister were killed. Somehow, Ms. Morgan was thrown from her bed and landed on the *Stockholm*, suffering only, a broken arm. The crew of the *Stockholm*, after examining their ship, realized it was not going to sink. The *Doria*, however, was damaged badly and was listing more than twenty degrees, which let seawater come into its compartments.

Even though help arrived quickly as it was a heavily trafficked sea-lane, things aboard were still perilous. Many of the people in the tourist section were trapped in their cabins. They had to brave smoke-filled hallways and knee-deep water. This is how Uncle Benny described it to us. When the *Doria* was hit, it knocked him to the floor in the main ballroom. He got up and made his way to the staircase going down to tourist class. Almost everyone was coming up. He, being a tall and powerfully built man, was able to push his way down. The water was up to his waist as he reached cabin 230. The jam around the door was twisted, and he couldn't open it. Several crew members were rushing by him, heading to the stairs. Despite his pleas for help, none would stop. He heard someone's horrific screaming in cabin 230! He kept trying to get it open to no avail. The hall was filling with smoke, and he was having a hard time breathing. Finally, being overwhelmed by smoke and not hearing anyone screaming anymore, he made his way up the stairs, and what he found was total chaos. As the ship was listing to the right, the main deck had a steep slippery slope. The lifeboats on the port side created many problems as they couldn't be launched. In order to get to the starboard-side lifeboats, most of the passengers, including Uncle Benny, had to lie on their backs and slide down the deck, hoping to stop before they went off the edge into the water.

Meanwhile, it was continuing to roll and threatening to capsize. At that point, Calamai was sure he would have to abandon the ship. But because the ship was listing so badly and the eight lifeboats could not be launched and the lifeboats on the starboard side could only hold one thousand of the passengers and crew who were on board, he decided not to abandon ship at that time. *Andrea Doria* radioed, "Need lifeboats as many as possible. Can't use our lifeboats." The *Stockholm* had already started rescuing people from the *Doria*. The first ship to arrive was a small freighter named *Cape Ann* at about 12:30 a.m. After that, two American navy ships arrived. However, none of them had many lifeboats.

Also receiving the emergency message was the French liner the *Île de France*, which had passed the area earlier in the evening heading to France. During the Second World War, it had carried 626,000 troops. After the war, it was completely overhauled and outfitted in 1949 and became known as a ship with gracious living. The *Île de France* was being captained by a fifty-three-year-old Barron Raul De Beurden who was a vacation replacement for the regular captain. The *France* at that time had 940 passengers and a crew of 826 on board. Upon receiving the emergency call, he turned the ship around and headed for the accident. About 2:00 a.m., the *France* came along the side of the *Doria*. It lit up the area with its floodlights and started dropping its lifeboats into the water, rescuing people who were swimming in the water. Uncle Benny was one of the rescued. When he saw the lifeboats, he worked his way down the side of the ship and jumped into the ocean and was rescued.

The rescue which was one of the largest in maritime history lasted until about 5:00 a.m. Nearly all the *Doria's* survivors had been evacuated. Seven hundred fifty-three were on the *France*, while the rest were on the *Stockholm* and four other ships. God only knows what an even greater catastrophe it would have been if the brave captain did not turn his ship around. Captain Calamai and a few officers were the last ones off. The *Doria* finally capsized and flooded. At 10:19 a.m., it sank into the Atlantic.

Captain Calamai initially said everyone was off the ship. I guess he should have said, "Except those fifty people who perished," which included my wonderful grandmother and my beautiful aunt Molly, Margaret Carola, her mother, and her siblings. Their two cabins took the direct hit. One person died at Roosevelt Hospital when she arrived in New York. There were many with bones that were shattered and with cuts and bruises. Five people on the *Stockholm* also perished.

Meanwhile, my mom, dad, aunts, and uncles had received calls from our family in Brooklyn saying that the *Andrea Doria* had been in an accident at sea and the people on board were being taken to New York and Boston. Mom and dad got dressed. I heard them leave without saying a word. I thought they were going to the ship to meet my grandmother and aunt and uncle. It wasn't until late in the morning they called to tell me the ship had been in an accident and they were waiting for the passengers to arrive on the other ships.

The Covino and Iazzetta families could do nothing but watch and pray as some small ships arrived with passengers. No sight however of our grandmother or aunt and uncle. In what seemed like an eternity to them, the two families waited and waited. Finally, the *France* appeared in the daylight, coming toward them. My aunt Rose told me what a "beautiful sight." When the *France* docked, people scanned every stretcher, searching for their loved ones. Then those that could walk on their own started to disembark. A sea of humanity was coming down the plank. It was to be almost seven hundred that were able to touch dry land to cheers and tears. Finally, the people from Brooklyn, as we always lovingly called them, saw Uncle Benny and let out cheers and whistles, calling and running toward him. He was disheveled and looked old and worn out. The first words out of his mouth were *sono morte*—they are dead. Everyone in both families became hysterical.

Cristina, her sister Molly and her husband, Benevenuto
Iazzetta taken by a professional photographer the night of
the sinking of the Andréa Doria—July 25, 1956

Sinking of the Andrea Doria along the coast of Nantucket, Massachusetts, bound for New York City. One of history's most infamous maritime disasters. Out of 1700 people aboard including the crew, only 51 died, 2 of those being my grandmother and great aunt.—July 25, 1956

CHAPTER 24

The Aftermath

OUR FAMILY WOULDN'T give up hope and went to the hospitals in New York to check if maybe they had amnesia and didn't know who they were. They got in touch with family we had on the north side of Boston and told them to check the hospitals where people from the crash were taken. For weeks we refused to accept the inevitable; they were gone.

My cousin Jerry Vale was singing at the Palmer House in Chicago at the time. He was called and told by his sister Tina what had happened. He was devastated—first his brother Bobby in a car accident in 1936 and now his grandmother and aunt in 1956 almost on the same day twenty years later. The grandchildren were overcome with emotion that, in some instances, lingers today with my sister, Joyce, Cousin Barbara, and myself.

Relatives and friends came to the store to offer their sympathies. Though we didn't have a body, they continued to come—all these people whose lives she touched, lending some money to buy homes or not to lose their homes during the Depression, helping some to pay their children's college tuition, or offering a sumptuous meal during hard winters when there was no work for most of her close friends. The thing most people talked to us about was her being there to listen when they asked her advice, never judging and always holding in confidence whatever they told her.

Those that seemed most devastated by her passing who came to the store to pay their respects were her Black oh-so-loyal customers. In some instances, months after the tragedy when they found out by word of mouth of her passing, they would say, "I just found out about Mom," some with tears in their eyes. Many were grown, hardened men and loving women. They spoke of "Mom," letting them have food on credit during the Depression. Not only the parents came but many of their children who were now grown. One woman told us about her husband being sentenced for murder. She had no formal education and didn't have enough money to feed her children properly. My grandma made extra of what she cooked for dinner every night and had Uncle Fred bring it to her and the children. This went on for several months until she found employment as a housekeeper in Scarsdale, New York. The cook there would give her food to take home. She said with a smile she was grateful, but it wasn't as good as Mom's. No one in the family knew about this except Grandma and Uncle Fred.

Another thing she would do was when one of her female customers had to work late, they would ask her if their children could stay at the store until they got home. They would come and do homework or read and be quiet as a mouse unless someone in the family talked to them first. Edward and his brother Arthur were two of the people that used to go to the store. I met him while I was at the dry cleaner's in Mount Vernon a few years ago. He was about my age, and we became friends when I was at the store at Grandma's. He told me about being able to go there to stay when he and his younger brother came out of school. He was now retired and had worked for the City of Mount Vernon. His brother was a doctor and working in North Carolina. He said to me, "I don't know what would have become of us if we didn't have Mom to go to."

This is just another one of many things that her customers highlighted whenever they spoke of the effect the store had on their lives. My grandmother would have, I'm sure, continued to make a positive effect on family members and friends alike. She had her life cut short by the tragedy of the *Andrea Doria*. Her guidance and strong hand while alive will be felt for many years to come. Grandma, I love you so!

In Memory card: Cristina Covino and her
sister Amelia (aka Molly) Iazzetta

Back of memory card

EPILOGUE

AUNT OLGA TOOK over the business and tried to continue in Grandma's ways. However, it just wasn't to be. She bought more real estate and sold the rest of the lots next to the store. Many cousins would go to the store and fill up their cars with free groceries. But Grandma just wasn't there. Family parties stopped at the store.

Then, along came Peter Gimbel, heir to Gimbels department stores, who was an investment banker. He was also a professional deep-sea explorer. He had been the first to dive the wreck a mere twenty-eight hours after it sank. However, it was in 240 feet of murky water, and he wasn't successful. He needed better and more equipment. He decided to reach out to the people that survived and especially those who lost loved ones. He had maps of the ship and where the rooms were. Mr. Gimbel needed money, plain and simple, to go down to the *Doria* again. This, needless to say, excited the family. Our attorney checked him out and found he was very reputable. As Aunt Olga was the executor of Grandma's will, she decided to contribute to his next exploration, hoping to have a body or at least something that was with her at the time. A short time later after receiving several thousand dollars from our family and getting other donations, Mr. Gimbel started his exploration of the ship. The depth and severe currents made it impossible to complete his mission. There was not equipment in the 1950s that is available today. He went back three more times over the next twenty-five years. Sixteen people have died since 1956 trying to explore the ship. Again, it is because of poor visibility and unpredictable currents.

Trying so hard to at least keep Grandma's memory alive, Aunt Olga donated money to a Catholic hospital that was being built in the Bronx. This hospital was called Misericordia on East 233rd Street. The baby nursery at the hospital was dedicated to Grandma, and a plaque was put above the window with her name on it. My two children were born there. The name of the hospital was changed and is now Montefiore.

The estate also donated two stained-glass windows to Our Lady of Mount Carmel in honor of Grandma and Uncle Nick who had died a short time after her. Father Paul was a priest who solicited these items. He was a close friend of the family and was the pastor. Many of my cousins' and sister's children attended the grammar school there, and the parents worked very hard to make the school a success. My cousin Fannie's Tina had her brother Jerry Vale appear when he was in New York on a singing engagement at the Copa to help raise money for the school.

Meanwhile, a lawsuit had been filed by a large maritime law company on behalf of those hurt and deceased. After a time, this suit was settled, and the family got $9,000 for our Grandma's death. Many of the plaintiffs in the case felt they had been sold out by this big shot law firm. As I have looked over the facts over the years, I must agree with them. There was such glaring negligence by both ship's captains.

As Aunt Olga continued the business in the early sixties, she tried to satisfy all the nieces and nephews as best as she could. There were some who felt they didn't get enough of the pie. Some she helped fix their existing homes by giving large amounts of money. Those that didn't have homes were living in apartments in the homes that she was the owner of. She charged those nieces and nephews nominal rent. Their responsibility was to keep the property in good physical condition and to make sure all was well with the tenants. That was because following in Grandma's footsteps, Aunt Olga bought all multifamily homes. At one time, there were ten homes all in all. She was able to keep a record of how they were doing by keeping every bill for anything that was bought for each home down to the nuts and bolts. She also recorded all the rents, and it was put into her income tax statements. She kept, as I said earlier, meticulous records. How a person could do all that by herself and still run a separate business was unbelievable. I guess the apple didn't fall far from the tree. To tell you of the inner strengths that all the Covino girls had—genes of their mother—would be a book in itself.

In 1960, with gambling in Mount Vernon out of control, the Westchester District Attorney's Office subpoenaed all the known bookies in the city. Their reason was to try and get evidence that the police force was corrupt. Aunt Olga was the only woman there, along with several men. While sitting and waiting to be called, many of them were, as she told me, "shaking, tapping their feet, even one was sweating." Not my aunt! It seemed that one bookie was asking her too many questions, and she didn't like where they seemed to be going. It turned out later he was, shall we say, a cooperating witness.

My aunt said, "He was a piece of shit!" She divulged nothing to him, and she told me, "Because there was nothing." Even though I knew better.

When it was her turn to take the stand, the prosecutor said, "You are a known bookie in Mount Vernon." My aunt denied it. He said, "How, then, have you accumulated all the real estate you have?"

Aunt Olga replied that Grandma left it to her and the little she bought since Grandma's death was because she "ate beans three times a day."

The prosecutor said to the judge, "Your Honor, I am finished with this witness." That was that!

On another occasion in 1963, her builder, Joe, a heavy-set always-smiling man, was at the store to go over plans for one of the homes she had bought. A man knocked on the store door, which was locked as usual, saying he was sent by one of her customers, giving their name, to drop off a slip. Aunt Olga opened the door. He rushed in brandishing a gun! Wanting money, he was shaking and appeared to be on drugs. The mailman at the same time was approaching. She told the gunman to put away the gun so he wouldn't think anything was wrong. When he did this, Aunt Olga grabbed his hand and wouldn't let him get it out of his pocket and yelled at the mailman to call the police. Joe started to stutter, as he sometimes did, saying, "Olga, let him go." With that, Joe peed his pants. The young man finally pulled himself free and ran away.

When the police arrived, they took Aunt Olga to the police station to look at mug shots. She picked him out. The police said they knew of him and therefore what to expect as he had been arrested, believe it or not, sixteen times before. And the money he did get, he would spend it on drugs in New York City, and then would return. Sure enough a few days later, he was arrested as he got off the number 16 bus on the border of Mount Vernon and the Bronx. After a while, he was put on trial, with Aunt Olga pointing him out as the robber. He was given a fifteen-year sentence.

A short time after the robbery, I saw Joe, the builder who by the way was a great guy, and he said to me, "Your aunt is crazy." Then went on to describe what had happened.

"No, Joe, just a Covino woman," I replied!

My mother and Aunt Rose continued going to the store every day to help her with whatever she needed them to do. Aunt Rose passed away in 1998 at the age of ninety. My uncle Nick had passed away in 1958; he was fifty-two. My aunt Fannie in 1969; she was fifty-eight. Aunt Olga, in the winter of 2008 at the age of ninety-six, passed away at the store, refusing many times to sell it and move somewhere else even though she had long ago stopped taking numbers as legalized gambling had taken away most of the business and many of her customers had passed on. Although the material things were still available, no one could duplicate the love and respect we had for our grandmother. Aunt Olga tried, but it just wasn't to be.

When Grandma died, as I said in the beginning, "The glue that held our family so solidly together had dried up and been washed away by the currents of the Atlantic."

Two siblings sued—Uncle Nick and Aunt Fannie—feeling the will was forged and saying Grandma would never have left all she had to one child. Aunt Olga settled with them, but the lawsuit created hard feelings that some are still harboring today.

My mother, Lydia—mine and my sister's, Joyce's, rock—left us on August of 2015, She was one hundred and had all her senses to the end. Now, she has joined her brother and sisters who had a bond that was, while on this earth, unique. I have no doubt it will continue in the life after.

As you can see reading this book, I put a great deal of emphasis on the food we ate and the people that shared our table. Not only because those times were filled with enjoyment, it was the togetherness. That because of the current times we live in, I'm so sorry to see it almost all disappear.

I dedicate this book to my family, all of who were and, in many ways, are still a very important part of my life. I love you dearly. To all my cousins' children, thank you for calling me uncle! You'll never know what *respect* means to me! It brings me back to the respect and love your mothers and fathers showed me and I them in return. You can't put a price tag on that. God bless you all.

I was living this story long before there was ever an idea of writing about it. We knew that Grandma and the store was something we never talked about but whose memories and secrets will forever be embedded in our souls.

Vincent (Jimmy) & Lydia DeFillippo—September 30, 1962

Neil & Camille DeFillippo's wedding along with his parents
Vincent (Jimmy) & Lydia—September 30, 1962

Current photo of the Store which is now fully a residence.

ABOUT THE AUTHOR

NEIL DEFILLIPPO, AUTHOR, had a lust for life and learning as a young child that has continued until this day. He is the grandson of Emilio and Cristina Covino and Anello and Gianina DeFillippo. He inherited many of the traits of both sets of his grandparents. While growing up, he spent a vast amount of time with his grandmother Cristina at the store, learning from her that grit and hard work most of the time would be rewarded.

As a young man, he went into the dry cleaning business which he made into a success and, at about the same time, opened fast-food restaurants with his cousin Jerry Vale, a very popular singer at the time. While Neil was in his forties, he got involved, along with two close friends, in the trotting horse race business, taking control of the day-to-day running of that enterprise, which became a profitable venture.

At the age of fifty-one while still controlling his businesses, he went back to school in the evenings to learn about the history of Italy. At fifty-four years of age, he went to

Pace University again in the evenings after working twelve-hour days to study history, which had been a passion of his since childhood.

Now, as a novice writer, he has written, with the help of many people, the incredible story of his grandmother Cristina and the store.